Bedtime Poems
for the
Mourning Soul

"A collection of melodic rhyming versus
to help entertain your mind
and soothe your soul."

Published by
MemorialGiftShop.com

Contents

INTRODUCTION

Bedtime Poems for the Mourning Soul takes the difficult and painful subject of death and helps to transform it into a celebration of life. It was written with love and takes you on an entertaining journey into a world of guardian angels, soul mates, fairies and more. The simple melodic rhyming poems, short stories and inspirational messages are easy and fun to read at bedtime, or anytime in order to help entertain your mind, while nourishing and soothing your soul.

Death is a part of life, and it affects us all. Whether it's the loss of a loved one, family member, friend, acquaintance, a public figure, favorite celebrity or lamenting the deaths you read or hear about in the news, we all are in mourning at times. It doesn't really matter if the loss was long ago or recent. The negative feelings associated with death can leave a lasting impression on our lives. Even if we are not aware of it, thoughts can manifest as feelings of sadness, guilt, anger, loneliness, helplessness and more. Hiding or suppressing these emotions when they arise can also lead to depression and numbness, robbing one's life of some of the happiness and fulfillment as well as affect their health negatively. So, most of the poems in this book have happy endings, in order to bring some peace and calmness back into your life. I also added some poems with advice to help you through the grieving process. I hope this book not only entertains you but brings you some comfort for yourself, a family member, friend or loved one.

Guardian Angel

I am a Guardian Angel

Sent from heaven above

I bring to you my blessings

And an abundance of my love

I will wrap my wings around you

Or lift you up when you're in need

I will attract good things into your life

Because I want you to succeed

I breathe in your goals and prayers

And exhale your wishes and desires

So, give me your worries and cares

And look at what transpires

Have faith that with time

Things will be alright

I am with you during the day

and all throughout the night

Do Not Weep

Do not weep,

I am next to you,

rest upon your pillow and into a restful sleep.

Can you hear my voice in the wind?

Can you see my silhouette glisten in the sun?

I am in your dreams too.

All is fine,

Dream of a beautiful dream,

dance in a field of flowers,

place your feet in a calm stream.

Take a ride in the breeze,

float in a cloud,

do what you please.

Whenever you need me,

I'll be at your side,

day or night.

I am here,

a guiding light.

The Peace Within

Sometimes the best way to see
IS TO CLOSE YOUR EYES
To not question everything and
PUT AWAY THE WHYS
To rise above the clouds
IN YOUR MIND
so, you'll be gently reminded and
YOUR EYES WILL BEHOLD
that from which you've been blinded
THE PEACE AND FULFILLMENT
you want in your life to be
HAS ALWAYS BEEN WITHIN
it did not flee It shines within you
BRIGHT AS A STAR
That whom you want to be
YOU ALREADY ARE
The beauty and love within you are the things
THAT ARE REALLY TRUE

Fallen Love

When those we love suddenly fall, leaving us alone with what seems like nothing at all. When our hearts feel as if it's broken into a thousand pieces, And the sorrowful thoughts from us rarely ceases,

HOLD ON
For life is a wondrous thing.
HOLD ON
And wait for the goodness it will bring.
HOLD ON
There will be a day when again your heart does sing.
HOLD ON
Blessings are coming to you on an angel's wing.

Things may seem dark now and nothing feels true. But listen to life it's calling for you. Life is precious, life is grand, practice putting away the sadness, get up and make your stand. Do the things you wanted to do, save the time for lamenting when your life is through.

I Needed a Rest

I needed to rest,
I was too tired to go on.
I knew it was best,
To leave with the dawn.
There was nothing left to give,
I had to go please don't be sad.
I fought so hard to live,
I gave it all I had,
Though the life from me did drain,
I am now free from my pain,
I'm in a better place,
And this new life I embrace.
Please be happy for me,
Don't lament that I'm not here.
For although you cannot see,
My eyes do not tear.
No longer do I need to rest,
With excitement I journey on.
As if on a personal quest,
Towards a beautiful light I am drawn.

I Release the Hurt and Pain

I release hurt and pain to heal my heart. And

free myself of apprehension as I make a new

start. Because I know that whatever I want to

achieve, is possible when I choose to believe.

I live in a world with limitless possibilities. A world that emboldens and frees, frees me to create my own purpose when I am in doubt. And provides everything I need so I won't feel I'm without. I have lost much but there is still much to gain. As in this wonderful world I remain.

Enjoy Each Minute

Go ahead, keep an eye out for

rainbows in your view.

Believe that the sun is smiling,

and its smile is just for you.

It's okay to feel the world's your oyster,

and you're its pearl.

And to learn to see the blessings

and chances around you swirl.

Try to enjoy earth's playground

as we are only here for a while.

This is your life so live it

on your terms and in your own style.

Yes, it's your hour

so, live it with power.

It's your minute so revel in it.

Stars at Night

In the morning when I wake, I miss you.
In the evening when I sleep, I miss you.

I know that you're not really gone,
Just on the other side.
I know that you are there for me,
But it feels like a part of me has died.
When you left, you left a large whole in my heart.
When you left, my mind couldn't comprehend,
that you really did depart.

A whirlwind of sadness,
surrounds me and holds me still.
A tornado of madness,
Rips to shreds my heart at will.

So, I do things that helps brings me peace,
Like counting the stars at night.
They calm my soul
and seem to give to me
An inner light

Is Seeing Believing?

You cannot see the air, but you can breathe it.

You cannot see the water, but you can taste it.

You cannot see the wind, yet you feel it.

There are colors before your eyes, yet you cannot see them all.

There are sounds all around but upon your ears not all fall.

Still…You say, "I'll believe it when I see it?"

Sparkling Light

Glorious little sparkling light,

seemingly floating in the air,

are you an angel in disguise,

bringing hope to those in despair?

With a light so pure it could pierce

the darkest veil,

making even the brightest star,

compared to you look pale.

Shine your light on sadness

to dry up all the tears.

Shine your light on insecurities

to dissipate all the fears.

Resonate in and illuminate

hearts and minds everywhere.

Fill the world with happiness, hope and care.

Supporting Each Other

When it comes to grief it's not about getting over it, it's about learning to handle it in a way that brings you long term relief. And, while the grief changes us, it also teaches us things that before we did not know. It can teach us to accept things, and how to let some things go. Grief can sculpt us into someone who has a profound understanding and appreciation of life. As we learn firsthand what it is to lose a life. We understand and have felt that pain that cuts like a knife. And through our sorrow we are better able to help another. Coming together to grieve and support each other.

Letting Go of Fear

I am letting go of my fears,

I am letting go of my tears,

I am letting go of the pain,

I am letting go to live again.

I am letting go to bring me peace.

I am letting go to bring release.

I am letting go of all that saddens,

I am making room for all that gladdens,

These things I do help end the sorrow.

These things I do for a brighter tomorrow.

I Am in Control of My Emotions

I am in control of my emotions.

My emotions do not control me.

I am in control of my emotions.

And from them I do not flee.

I can choose to mourn and grieve.

I can choose how best my pain to relieve.

No need to hide from emotions or leave.

Nor to my emotions do I need to cleave.

However, I choose to express my sorrow,

Is time well spent today and for tomorrow.

So, I experience the feelings I feel I must.

Because in my ability to heal I trust.

Therefore, try not to fear the negative,

Simply see it as a vehicle for change

and go through the barriers

changing things to "I will" from "I won't."

Keep moving through each obstacle

And greet each challenge

as a chance to grow.

And share what you learn with others you know.

CREATE your own rainbow EVERYDAY

Leave Behind the Rain

Do not over wallow in your sorrow or grief.

From your own strings from time to time cut some relief.

Learn to fly again.

To hold your head up high.

Breathe in the joy and exhale the mournful sigh.

Leave behind the rain.

Fly towards the light of the sun.

Rise to the challenges each new day will bring.

Listen to the melody that your heart will sing.

Feel the love that surrounds?

See the goodness all around?

You can see it if you choose.

Yes, you have lost much, but, yourself you did not lose.

It's okay to let go of your worries and pain.

To allow the sun within you to shine

and see the rainbows after the rain.

My Friend and I

When family and friends ask me whom I love,

I tell them some women marry men,

some marry women,

some marry no one at all.

I chose my friend and I feel that I made the right call.

Together, happiness my friend and I do chase.

As we travel together from place to place.

We encourage each other our dreams to pursue.

And seldom do we quarrel or argue.

We are never lonely, or lacking care.

We have lots of love and with the world we share.

A better person for myself couldn't be.

My friend always brings out the best in me.

We've been together from beginning to end.

My friend is myself and I am my friend.

Happiness Deserved

I deserve to be happy and enjoy life more.

So, one foot in front of the other

I choose to walk out the door.

Into the light, into the world so grand.

And, here in the light I will make my stand.

I choose to live my life to the fullest each day.

You are here in my heart and so together we stay.

With you I feel the strength to live my life full.

No needing to push myself I can feel life's pull.

I can now greet each day with a happy smile.

For you have been with me all the while.

I Found an Angel

I saw a shiny gold coin upon the street.
Just lying there waiting for me to meet.
And upon that coin that I picked up.
Was a picture of an angel holding a small cup.
I couldn't help to pause and think it peculiar.
Such an odd picture but strangely familiar.
Just then my brain fed my head with selfish desires.
You know, the kind of thoughts that lead mere
mortals to the fire.

This voice stated that I should take this angel coin to
the pawn shop.
Or to my favorite pub and with the bartender to swap.
I wondered how many mugs of brew a shiny gold
coin would fetch.
Possibly a hundred…but that might be a stretch.

Then my conscious in a softer voice I've heard many
times before,
stated that the richness I was feeling would only
make me poor.
It said this little angel has been with me all along.
And by my side, it really did belong.
It said when you picked up the coin laying on the
street.
It was because life's timing was perfect, on beat.

You're stopping to look at it laying by your feet,
caused you to miss that mugger walking down the
street.

And yesterday when you looked at its outline in the
clouds in the sky,
It caused you to miss a car that went whizzing by.
Soon believing my conscious might be a guiding light
I couldn't see,
I set the golden coin down on the ground to the side
of me.

My mind chimed in, "what in the hell are you doing?
You know your conscious with you is only screwing!"
It said, "What kind of guy would place a golden coin
upon the ground? Especially with so many poor
people all around?"

Then my conscious said to my surprise.
Don't take offense but your minds an idiot and it's full
of lies.
So, I pondered for a moment, and I decided to place
the gold coin into the cup of a beggar down the
street.
And watched the angel fly away till another day we'd
meet.

HOMELESS
PL...
HEL...

Quiet Your Mind

To keep you grounded you've been given a mind.
Its tensely twisted and difficult to unwind. But never
forget it's the true you that pulls the strings. The true
you can override its programming's. Your mind gives
meaning, but for your soul it's just a cart. It feeds you
information but from the real you it's not a part. So
never, ever let your mind become your jail. Because
for a dollar it might put your soul on sale. The mind
can sometimes be lazy and oh so weak, you need to
constantly push it if its truth you seek. Remember
you are the spark that gives life to every brain cell.
Your mind is like a dog, but your Pavlov with the bell.

You Have the Power of Acceptance

You can assent your grief when you see fit. By accepting the situation and rising above it. First you need to realize that death is a natural process of life. It's not something in your life to just cause more strife. Once you can accept this and let go of things you cannot rearrange. Your life gains power and you are free to go on or make a needed change. And while all this seems easy to do it is often hard. For its in our nature not to give up or let down our guard. But acceptance is one of the final stages of grief. And it is one of the stages that brings the greatest relief.

No Time for Regrets

Some feast on regrets when they really should not partake,

Regrets can turn precious time into years of heartache.

Regrets will steal your life away,

Save the "could of", "would of" and "should of" for a rainy day.

So, stop whining, defining, confining, just let yourself be,

Whatever it is that sets your heart free.

No hesitating, no debating,

less concentrating and waiting.

Take the chances that you get,

if you make a mistake, please don't fret.

One person's imperfection,

is often another person's direction.

It's how you perceive,

And what you believe,

That measures what you achieve.

Just do what you believe needs to be done,

and smell the roses and have some fun.

Remember you are the perfect you just as you are,

This is your life and you're the star.

Overcoming the Obstacles

You can say things like this to bring some relief to your grief…

I can overcome every obstacle and roadblock. I found the key and my heart I unlock. My mind is clearer, and I am ready to begin. I am happy and ready for a new show to be in. I am the actor and can write my own play. I can do the things that I've always wanted to do. Because within me is the strength that comes from you. You would want me to be happy and to wipe away the tears. To celebrate your life by living fully and not waste away the years.

No More Sad Songs

I used to dance to only sad songs.
They were my friend,
From beginning to end,
I knew them all by heart.

Then came you,
you didn't like the sad songs.
You said I am in for a treat,
Showed me a brand-new beat,
A melody that touched my heart,
Gave me a brand-new start,
That lifted me out of my chair,
Without a worry or care.

Now I won't dance to any sad songs,
I've heard them all before,
Ain't going to dance no more,
Until that sad song ends.

So, DJ please don't play me any sad songs.
If you want me on the floor, play a happy beat,
To get me on my feet,
Cause I ain't going to dance no more,
Until that sad song ends.

Leaning on Others

It's very easy to just put aside you're your feelings to bring yourself some relief, from your grief. But that is only a temporary band aid. The pain and sadness are still there, it's only delayed. The pent-up emotions can end up causing havoc in your life and causing you depression or other unneeded strife. Dragging around sometimes years hidden pain and hurt. In the long run will take more energy to exert. And by telling everyone around you're okay, you're pretty much just telling them to stay away. A strong support network is much to be desired, it's good to lean on others when you're feeling overwhelmed and tired.

HEALING TAKES TIME AND SELF♥CARE

Time to Heal

Tick tock, tick tock…

I am taking my time to grieve.

Tick tock, tick tock…

I am taking my time to sorrow.

Tick tock, tick tock…

I am taking my time to mourn.

Tick tock, tick tock…

I am taking some time to feel sadness.

Tick tock, tick tock…

And when tomorrow the new day brings….

I am taking my time to rejoice.

Tick tock, tick tock…

I am taking my time to feel happiness.

Tick tock, tick tock…

I am taking my time to celebrate life.

Tick tock, tick tock…

I am taking my time to appreciate the small things.

Tick tock, tick tock…

Goes the clock as I grow in strength each day,

As time heals my heart and takes the pain away.

Ebb & Tide

The spirit of love is ever so near,

When you're in my arms.

The spirit of love is my one true dear,

And to my heart carries the charms.

Upon angel wings our spirits soar,

Above all our worries and cares.

Upon angel wings with the one I adore,

We make such a perfect pair.

Joined in flight, joined by soul,

Intertwined in faith and love.

Joined by heart, joined in full,

A soaring eagle and a peace dove.

An adventurous pair we do make,

Completing and complementing each other.

Choosing to be side by side,

Creating memories and experiencing life,

As we fly freely in life's ebb and tide.

Nobody is Perfect

Nobody is perfect, no, not even them.

Flaws and imperfections are stitched into us in our

hem.

We all arrive shiny and new in our birthday suits.

But in time they get soiled and wrinkled as we

struggle to plant our roots.

Sometimes others impact us negatively as they send out their own shoots.

If we are weak, we allow ourselves to be overtaken in the garden.

When others bother us it's easy to give in or snap in anger without a pardon.

There is a fine balance between being too weak or too strong.

Actions and words can hurt, and their effects felt lifelong.

So, learn to just forgive the people in your life for which you care.

And if you must with others it's okay to just to just spread your own roots elsewhere.

Pluck the weeds in your garden, pluck them from your life.

Because life is too short to handle the unwanted burdens of unwanted strife.

Again, nobody is perfect, no, not even them.

All you can really do is wash your own clothes and mend your tattered hem.

Remember how shiny and new your birthday suit once was.

Strive to forgive and don't worry so much about what someone else does.

What is Coping

Coping is simply doing what you can to help deal with grief. It's the active process of doing things you feel will bring you the most relief. You can read books, go to a support group, talk to family or a friend. There are also lots of tools to assist in order to help you transcend. You can meditate or take up a new hobby if you like. The key is to help eliminate the stress in order to improve your psyche. When you neutralize the stressors your utilizing great strategies, That will help your mind and body to feel more at ease.

Money and Charity

And the old lady said…

I want money because I'm tired of being a charity.

I want money because in my life it's such a rarity.

Yes, I want money, lots and lots of money.

Because in this world, money is like honey.

It sweetens everything and makes life sunny.

Yes, indeed what I want is a whole lot more money.

I need it for what I endeavor.

With money I can be oh so clever.

Please God, make my life complete.

Make my life really, really, sweet.

It's a big, big world, and I'm tired of the fall.

I'm tired of waiting for happiness, I want it all.

Her guardian angel obedient to her word,

Delivered the message to heaven that he had heard.

A voice from heaven replied…

"I will grant one wish, said a voice to the guardian

angel with a sigh. But alas, unfortunately she's got

cancer, and in weeks she will die. She doesn't even realize that she is sick. But it will consume her body ever so quick. I thought about giving her more time on a platter. But this wish for so much money shows me what to her really matters. If she spends the money on herself there isn't a doubt. She may not be going to the good place as, the greedy and selfish tend to fall out."

The worried guardian angel pondered every word,
he wished he hadn't relayed the message he had
heard. He came down to the woman from above
and left a box of gold and a message wrote with love.

The woman entered the room and saw the box of
gold on the floor. She dove down saying I'm rich as
the gold coins through her hands did pour.
Then she stood up towards the stars in the sky.
She said thank you to the heavens without
questioning why. She sat down at the table to write a
list of everything she would buy. That's when she

found the angels note that made her cry. She picked
up the note and read it, and pondered a while, with
an awestruck smile. It seemed a lifetime ago,
but she could recognize the handwriting style.

A style of cursive writing that only he could pen.
Letters so sweet that they won her hand over all the
other men. But before they could marry, he went
home to meet his maker. As for this woman in
mourning, soon her hand in marriage had no more
takers.

As the tears streamed down her face, she could
remember his loving embrace. She dried the tears
and knew exactly what with the gold she should be
done. She found a charity and donated it in his name
and felt bright and warm as the sun.

But alas, within weeks the sun soon turned dark as
deaths chill set in. The cancer consumed her just as
her new life of philanthropy did begin. She died just

as the guardian angel had been told. She was too tired to get up and her body too sick and old.

Alone and broke in her apartment she breathed her last breath with no one there to grieve. But the life she gained in heaven with her true love was better than she could ever conceive.

Angel Thoughts

Do angels come from heaven,

Maybe a place close but far away?

Is it a land where everything moves at God speed?

Where a million years could be a day?

If an angel can travel through galaxies in just a minute,

Could it be that an angel lives outside of earth and within it?

Simultaneously doing works far and wide…

Yet finding the patience to sit and stay by someone's side.

Is an angel so small you can't see them at all?

And do they just wait for your beckon call?

As for me, I've never heard or seen one speak,

But it's fun to think about angels

when you have some time to think.

Sing to Me

Sing my angel so gently and kind.

Sing to open my eyes and my mind.

Sing to fill my days with goodness divine.

Sing to spread sunshine on me and mine.

Sing to make rights and for wrongs to mend.

Sing to bless my days from morning to end.

Sing until my head and pillow do meet.

Sing my angel so softly and sweet.

………

I'll sing to you with melodic rhyme.

I'll sing with angel choirs as bells chime.

I'll sing to you in heavenly harmonic tune.

I'll sing together with the stars and the moon.

I'll sing for your blessings and sing for prayers.

I'll sing for your faith and all your cares.

I'll sing for the sun for you to shine bright.

Now sleep as I sing throughout the night.

The Road Less Traveled

The road less traveled can be a heavy tread when you're all alone. But it's worth the effort at times if you can place your mind in the right zone. But be careful not to lose yourself inside of your own individuality. Cause over time you'll find that you can become merely what you think you ought to be. Lost inside your own reflection, you can lose your sense of direction. So be careful not to simply view others as an impedance. For often the lessons others have learned can give your own life more credence. And the learning from their own trials and tribulations, can help enlighten you and give you new revelations.

Love Never Dies

Love is a force that simply is

and through us it does flow

No need to hoard it, release it and let it go

It manifests in the kind deeds

and words we do

It strengthens our own being

while fortifying others too

It is our greatest armor

as it helps us to forgive and forget

And it can lift us up

even out of the darkest pit

So, fill your heart with love

Count your blessings from above

And you will feel happier as you

greet each new dawn

And remember love never dies

when you leave your heart light on

I Can Cope

(Say to yourself…)

I can cope with the grieving process.

Because I know in time I will grieve much less.

Each day I am feeling stronger by the hour.

Inside I can feel my own inner power.

I can handle the sorrow and the pain.

Because as I release it away it will drain.

I can already feel my heart begin to heal.

And in time it will be acceptance that I'll feel.

It's not a matter of hope,

I really know that I can cope.

Don't Force Your Strength

Don't force yourself to be too strong. Feeling weak in a situation you cannot control is not wrong. You may think that other people do not wish to see you crying. But it's only natural to be sad when you think about death and dying. Walking around as if nothing has happened may momentarily numb the pain. But it won't make you stronger as it's a façade you can't maintain. The stress on your mind and body can make you weaker, there's little to gain. Don't force your strength by pretending everything is okay. Just go through the grieving process and the sadness on its own will melt away.

Do Not Let Anger Dwell

Do not allow anger in your mind too long to dwell. In time it will only place your heart in a prison cell. Anger can be a natural response there is nothing to fear. Some people express it verbally, others with a tear. And when you feel its time and you want to let your anger go. Simply unlock the door to your heart and let your love flow. Allow the river of compassion to wash away any anger that resides, the more you give to others, the larger will be the tides. Allow the anger to flow away back into the ocean of emotion. Watch it depart to some faraway distant shore. As peace embraces you and calmness to your soul you restore.

Mourn Death as I Celebrate Life

It's okay that my heart feels lighter every day.

It's okay that my inner child wants to play.

It's okay to dance and sing

and to feel the joy life brings.

It's okay to think of happier things.

To realize each moment is precious on earth.

To see more clearly life's real worth.

Through tears I've learned that we are on this

planet for just a short while.

So, I will do more things that make me smile.

Yes, it's okay to be both sad and glad.

To mourn your death

and celebrate all that we had.

A Higher Love

Where the bluest blue ocean meets the shore,

Upon an island alone in the sea.

White sand sparkles like diamonds

the trade winds breeze through the trees.

The sunlight warms and caresses the skin.

Such a beautiful place to imagine

when I need some time within.

But there's one thing better, one more true,

The peace I find when I follow you.

With eyes wide open, looking towards your light,

I feel at home, everything turns right.

Only you can make a dark day turn bright.

Only you can surpass every earthly view.

Only you can make a life renew.

You lift me high above everything low,

Only you can make my heart glow.

Thank you for being by my side,

A guardian angel, a friend, a guide.

The Love and Support of Others

Take comfort in the love and support from others. The friends, relatives, sisters, brothers and mothers. For everyone has something they want to say. Most only are trying to help take your pain away. And for those whose words that may not help. That unintentionally strike your heart with a whelp. Realize that they probably cannot understand how it does hurt. When from their mouths an insensitive remark will spurt. Try to remember that in your mourning you may be more sensitive than most. And life more difficult, and the path not so easy to coast. Grief can be a bumpy ride filled with twists and turns. When your left without something for which your heart so yearns. You may pout, shout, or feel in doubt. But whatever your feeling, try not to lock everyone out. For some are like guiding lights. Their words can help make things feel more right. Be thankful for the support they give. And for those that make things a bit worse simply try to forgive.

Time To Start Living

I am ready to start living my life again.

It's not a matter if but when.

And when is now as I live in the present.

And I make this vow to make my life more pleasant.

To actively choose to do what is best for me.

To decisively choose to just let what is be.

So, I move forward with a brand-new beat.

I have so much left to do and goals to complete.

I just can't continue to wither and hide.

I gain strength knowing in my heart and thoughts,

You will always reside.

Game of Life

The game of life is the ultimate role game.

And for all who play, the rules are the same.

They are easy rules with no time limit.

If you lose a turn, you can jump back in it.

As soon as the dice are passed to you,

By trial and error, you learn what to do.

If plan 1 didn't work, next time try plan 2.

The more you roll. The more you grow.

If there is a path, you're unsure to take,

Create a new path for yourself and others sake.

Sometimes, moving forward is the hardest thing to do.

It requires body, mind and spirit to be true.

It's a three-legged race and all must be as one.

At times it's difficult, but sometimes can be fun.

If you're stuck in a maze build yourself a door.

If your blinded by wealth share it with the poor.

So, stop defining, confining, just let yourself be.

Whatever it is that sets your heart free.

No hesitating, no debating, less concentrating and waiting.

Take the chances that you get, if you make a mistake,

please don't fret.

Just do what you believe needs to be done and smell the

roses and have some fun.

It Will Be Okay

It will be okay, were the last words uttered from her lips.

It will be Okay? Okay! A shredded heart will never mend from

the rips.

I pondered the sound of her voice in that instant.

Not knowing then that it was me just being resistant.

Death's door flew open that day,

and in a rush tore her from my embrace.

A whirlwind of emotions, frantic thoughts,

yet barely enough time to gaze upon her face.

I left her there all alone and ran as far away as I could

as our world came tumbling down.

I should have stayed by her side,

I should have stayed I cried,

but deaths fear was overwhelming.

The smoke, the heat, the crumbling of the walls,

the screams and terror were all consuming.

I made it through the office door

and into the blackened hallway strewn with debris.

I stepped over several people laying upon the ground

as the confusion set upon me.

Where am I, what happened,

the smoke was both blinding and suffocating.

Disoriented and confused I fell down.

I then saw an open door with a light radiating.

I crawled towards the light

and there she was saying "It will be Okay."

Finding Strength

I am finding strength in myself as I grieve.

I'm filtering out the sadness

from the happiness like a sieve.

And the more happiness that I can retrieve.

The more happiness I'm able to perceive.

This adds more comfort in my life to relieve.

The feelings of loneliness and emptiness that

deceive.

Because things are actually

better than I can conceive.

As I know inside

I have the power to achieve

Everything I need

is within me if I choose to believe.

The Young Teen Prayed

"If I were an angel from above

I would blanket the world in love

I would pray for every sorrow

I would brighten every tomorrow

If I were an angel from above."

The angel hearing the sincere prayer

Of wanting to heal the world with care

Said, please don't underestimate your worth

Your needed where you are here on earth

You don't need wings on your back

Or an angel license on your wall to tack

You don't need a halo of gold or wear white

In order to help make the wrongs in the world right

One earth angel is worth 1000 in the sky

You can do so much, and you don't have to fly

You could be a teacher, doctor or nurse

A preacher or fireman it's so diverse

A policeman, volunteer, counselor too

There are thousands of jobs you could do

You can be a guardian angel to others in need

No need to apply your job is guaranteed

No Timelines

Get the timeline out of your head. There is no clear amount of time to grieve no matter what anyone said. Everyone is different and different they react. So don't listen when they say your grieving too much or little, because it's based upon their own fact. Let go of the expectations that you place on yourself to do as others do. Listen to your heart it will tell you when the mourning is through. You can't just get over grief because someone tells you to. The only person who can tell you when is you. This is your life, and your timeline is yours. You are free to retreat or to unlock the doors.

Guardian Angels Softly Chant

A lost soul's bitter cry,

As a white dove lays down to die.

All hope fades when love is dead,

All hope fades as hate spreads.

An angry mob in unison voice,

Demands vengeance as their choice.

A man of peace is laid to rest,

What he lived for is put to test.

As media outlets fuel the fire,

People speak in shock and ire.

The bridge he built is about to collapse,

Bad blood fuels another relapse.

Politicians watch in sadness,

As all their efforts are lost in madness.

Guardian Angels on both sides softly chant.

Better think twice before you start to fight.

One person's wrong is another person's right.

One person's victory is another's person's loss.

One person's sinner is another's person's cross.

There are no winners in the game of war.

So, what in the hell are you fighting for?

If you think you've won, you may have lost.

When you start to tally up the final cost.

Citizens on both sides quietly mourn.

Soldiers searching for missing souls,

Through valleys, over hills, in dugout holes.

Searching through bodies piled in a heap.

More and more soldiers arrive and weep.

The soldier's numbers keep multiplying.

More and more souls fall down crying.

Kneeling beside victims with ghostly stare,

Watching themselves lying there.

I Am with You

Do not despair or sorrow

For even though I won't be with you tomorrow

I am with you

Death has not changed me

Even though you can't see

I am with you

Time doesn't really change things

Each night still the day brings

I am with you

It's all as they once were

There is nothing for us to endure

I am with you

Call me by my name

Talk to me when you need me

I am with you

Do not hide me away

Do not from our memories stray

I am with you

A Job Well Done

And the old man said…

I have shed a million tears
Carried regrets through the years

I have toiled and have tainted
Till my insides nearly fainted!

Fame, fortune and love still to elude me,
I'm still nowhere nearer to each

Where is the path which I should be?
What is that I should strive to reach?

Am I just chasing my own tail wasting time?
For a paltry nickel or a quick dime.
How long must I wait for the sublime?
Such a fool the clock of me must chime.

Now tell me angel, my good friend,

As my time here on earth nears its end.

Did I do a job well done?
Did I work too much or have too much fun?

Should I grieve in sorrow?
Or in hope, ask for another tomorrow?

What to do?
When your life is nearly through?

Said the angel to the old man,
take my hand, and understand,
all you could do is what you can.

Look past the self-inflicted expectations and chatters,
and the regrets that only batters.

Your inner battle has been won.
All you needed to do, has already done.

You Have Psychological Resilience

Within you resides the power to succeed, it's a strong

force that you can use as you need. You have the

psychological resilience to cope and adapt, it's a gift

that fortifies your strength when you are feeling

trapped. You have the capability that allows you to

remain calm. When a crisis happens in your life you

know how to put on the balm. You can use it to help

erase your problems and stress. And move on with

lessons learned with each success. You are

mentally strong and capable too. And the more you

believe in yourself, the more you will be able to do.

Rise Above the Clouds

Rise above the clouds in your mind

so, you'll be gently reminded.

And your eyes will clearly see what is true.

The beauty and love that resides within you.

Your heart is sacred ground.

its where goodness is found.

It's a place where hope springs eternal.

Or a spark can turn infernal.

It is the lightness, your very air.

It can erase every worry, replacing it with care.

So, try not to worry or think so much.

Thoughts can lead you astray and out of touch.

Dwell in your heart with love and hope,

And you'll always have the tools within to cope.

6
Letting Go is a Part of Life

Letting go is a part of life I know. People come into our lives and often to help us grow. And when they leave us, they leave a part of them. Along with a pearl of wisdom like a hidden gem. So, I have learned to appreciate all whom pass my way. Regardless of if with me they are not able to stay. And if they depart this world for another, I choose to be happy that for a while we had each other.

Never Be the Same

You were born into a world
of constant change,
One day everything familiar,
the next can seem oh so strange.
Time stands still for no one
we all can agree,
We are constantly evolving
personally and planetarily.

However, there is a way
to preserve moments lost,
An easy way to make time stand still
without any cost.
Cherish the memories
and to them hold on tight.
They can bring comfort
throughout the day and night.

Things will never be the same
that's just how things are.
But memories can stand still
no matter how near or far.

Thankful for the Moments

When we met in the hospital,
we were both sprouting wings
and away I thought we'd soon fly.
But then love struck and I dared
not question why.

I embraced and cherished you,
and being together was my only care.
Me with my tubes and you with your
robe and wheelchair,
aaahhh… we made such a beautiful pair.

A few short months is all it took
to fall deeply in love with you.
It was a few short months of love
that made every cell in my body feel anew.

Now it's a few short years later,
and I don't dare question how or why.
We are both here on earth still, no wings yet,
but how our hearts do fly!

Exercise Away the Grief

When your emotions are high and your full of angst and stress, try exercising as it will help make your worries less. The physical endurance of exercise can help take your focus off your emotional pain, and the health benefits of exercise are a positive gain. Physical activity helps to releases brain chemicals like endorphins and such. These can help relieve discomfort and boost your moods much. The movement of these neurotransmitters is a positive to also prevent depression. Engaging in exercise can help focus your mind and come to surface things under suppression. Exercise helps you gain back control in your life as you control your own body and mind. Giving you the space and time to concentrate on something physical and from grief rewind. It could be a short walk or run, yoga or Pilates, an activity or sport. You can do it alone every day, go to a gym or find a personal trainer to give you support.

Glory to the Earth

All life is wondrous and beautiful if you choose to see it.
Imagining the glory of all it all helps your mind conceive it.
When you transform your worries and cares
into thoughts of love and care.
Often, you'll find that what once was a problem
suddenly is not there.

Try It.

Imagine that high above your worries and cares is an angel divine, shining a white guiding light upon the world as it twirls amongst the stars. And all the angels stopped and gazed upon the planet saying, "you're beautiful and perfect, just the way you are." Can you imagine them there protecting you, surrounding you with love and care? Simply because you are a part of this magnificent creation called Earth that we all are blessed to share. Now imagine the angels dancing around in the shadows of the earth with awe and wonder. Singing songs of praise and encouragement for all on the planet with a melodic roaring thunder. For them all life is a miracle and precious from the smallest microbe to the biggest whale. All life is magnificent they say as through the clouds they sail.

Or think of something else
that brings your thoughts from low to high.
The point is simply to take a break from sorrow
And to your worries and troubles say goodbye.

Time to Grieve

I allow myself to grieve

then move on.

For tomorrow will bring

a brand-new dawn.

A new chance to handle things

in my own way.

A brighter tomorrow

pushing the sadness away.

Grieving is a natural process

to go through.

It will help me get over

the loss of losing you.

I allow myself to grieve

then move on.

Your Own Stages

Most everybody knows about the stages of grief. But you don't
have to follow them or even go through all of them so breathe
a sigh of relief. Denial, anger, bargaining, depression and
acceptance are the norm. But variations of these you can
easily form. You might also go through some out of order, but,
if it's right for you it's not disorder. Just know in your mind and
your heart that everything will be alright. And if you can reach
some type of acceptance things will seem more bright.

Cry if You Want To

Cry if you want to it's okay. There's no limit to how many tears a person can cry anyway. Even if they become dry tears, they will help wash away the sorrow. So go ahead and cry it's a coping mechanism that's free to borrow. There is really nothing weak about crying over the dead. It's nothing to avoid, nothing to dread. Crying tears won't keep you from healing or getting better. The worse that can happen is your cheeks will get wetter. But if you don't want to cry, don't cry at all. It's not necessary it's really your call. You can feel profound soundness without shedding a tear. Not crying is not something to fear. So, cry if you want or don't it's up to you. Just do what you need to, not what you think you must do.

Optimistically New

There are tools to help you when you are ready to let go, and they are just a few sentences away. Make up some like the ones below, they are easy to remember and say…

"I am optimistic about the new phase in my life now.
Not sure when it happened or even how.
I was simply mourning you each day.
When suddenly the sorrow drifted away.
Perhaps you had a hand in taking away the pain.
Perhaps it was only causing you disdain.
But however, it happened I'm glad it is done.
For it's time to come out and live in the sun.
To feel the power in each hour for a while.
To show my happiness with a large smile.
To celebrate your life without sacrificing mine.
I am accepting what is and feeling more divine."

It really doesn't matter the words you use when you write yourself a message of love. Just let the words embrace you and they will come to you like a peace dove.

Angelic Lessons

And the Guardian said to the new angel…

So that you can see that my message is sincere and real, I will put on my halo and give an angelic angel spiel. I tell you honestly and frankly that the things that you have done, have made things worse in the long run. I sincerely suggest you follow my lead and put some wings upon your back. Now go on, and fly away before I take my halo off, said the guardian angel with an angry scoff.

And the new angel said …

The new angel put on his wings and held his head down low, then said these words as he pointed to a spot beneath him on planet earth to show.

*I've been carefully setting things up; my mission is not done. Look closely at that person as he reaches down to pick up that dollar. Now look at the guy on the crane give out a great big holler. The chain broke loose the man bent down and his life was saved. And watch what happens next on this road I've paved. He then gives the dollar to that homeless veteran who lives on that street. Whom goes to that store there to buy himself something tasty to eat. He then goes back sits on the ground to eat as the parade passes by, now watch as he turns his head and sees that cardboard box from the corner of his eye. He gets up, opens it, now cover your ears as he screams… **"It's a bomb!"** The pedestrians were averted, and the authorities were all alerted, then the new angel sadly asserted, I know that there is no rebuttal, a guardian angel*

And the Guardian Angel replied…

Nonsense, even us Guardian angels are not perfect, we

cannot always predict and often there is conflict. Therefore,

sometimes you need to just let things be, as you grow wiser

into the future you will learn to better see.

The man who picked up that dollar, you saved his life from the

crane indeed. But he was the man who built the bomb, and

his soul was already lost to greed. He placed that box on the

sidewalk close to the store, He will now go on making dozens

more.

Then, the Guardian angel took off his halo and said…

"I admit I am also guilty of interfering." When the chain broke

on the crane, it was me who was steering. A Guardian Angel

should never take a life. So, you see even angels can suffer and strife. Now go on my friend and find more good things to

do, said the Guardian angel as away he flew.

In My Grief I Have Changed

In my grief I have changed.

What once was is now estranged.

Nothing is as it was before.

I am myself but from myself I tore.

It's as if a part of me is still with you.

It's hard to accept that your life is through.

I know in time that I will feel myself again.

I know it's not a matter of if but when.

I will piece myself back together and mend.

But don't worry about me my dear friend.

For in my grief I have also grown.

I am a stronger person

Because of the love you've shown.

It's a Good Day

It's a good day.

If the sun is in the sky.

It's a good day,

If the birds above you fly.

It's a good day.

If it's even when it's pouring down rain,

It's a good day.

No reason to complain,

It's a good day,

For writing down goals.

It's a good day,

For talking to your soul.

It's a good day,

For wishing upon a star.

It's a good day,

For being whom you are.

It's a good day!

So put some pep in your step,

Replace the no's, with a yep.

It's a good day!

May You Hear Them

- ✓ May they wipe away all your tears.
- ✓ May they give you a warm embrace.
- ✓ May they wipe away all your fears.
- ✓ May they take your worries and erase.
- ✓ May you feel the love they bring.
- ✓ May they fill your life with grace.
- ✓ May they bring you comfort and hope.
- ✓ May they bring tranquility to your mind.
- ✓ May they give you the tools to cope.
- ✓ May they unshackle the chains that bind.
- ✓ May they fill your life with happiness and joy.
- ✓ May they fill your heart with love and peace.
- ✓ May they give you many reasons to enjoy.
- ✓ May their blessings upon you release.
- ✓ All these things I want for you.
- ✓ All these things I pray they do.

Clarity of Thought

I will wake up tomorrow with clarity of thought.
I will make the decisions which I think I ought.
I will reassess the things that
in the past I have bought.
I will give away those things
that have caused nothing but fraught.
I will let go of the things
which have helped me naught.
I will gain strength from the lessons
I have been taught.
I will do this to help the worries
and troubles to be forgot.
I will do this to help bring me closer to
the happiness I sought.
I will continue a path that
my heart does plot.
I will continue a path that
causes my soul to dance a lot.
I will look forward to a new day
and give it my best shot.

I Trust My Soul

I trust and allow my soul

to help me create

a life happy and whole.

I trust my heart

to provide me with love.

I trust my mind

to give me wisdom from above.

I trust that everything

will turn out right.

As I turn off the light

and say goodnight.

Tomorrow is a new day

And I trust everything

Will be okay.

No Right or Wrong Way to Feel

There is no right or wrong to feel

the feelings I have within.

Feelings are a natural part of me

and help the healing begin.

I can be happy and optimistic.

In the face of sadness and negativity.

No matter the heaviness

or the situations gravity.

I can also be sorrowful and pessimistic if I choose.

Or be however I need to be to diffuse.

I can even choose to infuse my feelings if need be.

I give myself permission to feel how I feel

in order to set myself free.

Conception of the Human Race

Since the conception

of the human race,

So many have come before me,

too many to even trace.

And a part of who I am

is a part of whom they were.

I am their hope, there vision,

the dreams they confer.

So, with great honor

and reverence for the past,

I am grateful to just be alive

in this world so vast.

Living side by side

with relatives near and far.

All living together

in this grand bazaar

Youth Abandoned

And the old lady said in her dream…
I was a young person with stars in my eyes. I believed in
everything, of endless possibilities and wished upon the stars
in the skies. By my side I was cared for by an angel mild and
pure. My angel protected me and administered the cure.
For all that would spoil me, make me selfish and insecure. But
as I grew older, I thought I knew the meaning of it all, I treated
others as if they were at my beckon call. I didn't care about
angels, or anyone it's true. Everyone disappointed me, and
away my angel flew.

And a quiet voice calmly spoke to her…
I am lifting the veil of bitterness that envelopes thee. There's
your Guardian angel it always been here you see. And see all
those people who care? Some you haven't even met yet, but
don't worry they are there. I give you this choice now, you can
remain asleep in your bed. Or, by your guardian angel away
be lovingly led. You can be as a young person again with
stars in your eyes. Believing in everything, in a world of
possibilities it's yours if you try. If you want peace from your
body racked with pain. I can give you the release and a new
life you will gain.

The old lady paused then replied…
 "No way! Not even for a minute." With the veil gone now I can
again see this world and the goodness within it." I'm choosing
to live a few years more. To live fully and not drown in my
tears. I'm choosing my own path and not living in remorse and
fears. The alarm went off, and she woke up again. And while
she didn't remember her dream. She was happier than
before, and her eyes had a new gleam. She lived her life more
fully and worries she did release. Her life was better with her
newfound sense of peace.

Hold on to Love Let Go of Grief

I hold on to love

as I let go of grief.

I do this in order to help

bring a little relief.

It does not mean that I don't

miss you because I do.

It's just that too much missing

can make a heart turn blue.

I hope your life in heaven

brings you comfort and peace.

And please know that throughout my life

my love for you won't cease.

Love After Love

Saddened, she held her breath and did not say…

I cannot be without your love today,

I cannot exist without your love to stay.

You are the part of me that is the best of me.

You are the part of me that makes me feel free.

Then as dusk turned to dawn…

Her true love was gone.

A grief struck woman tried to move on.

With a fervent passion to write her wrong.

So, she made a promise with a heartfelt song.

Faithfully, my heart remains,
Faithfully, my heart refrains,
From love, from laughter, from everything,
That's dear to me until you bring,
Your love back to me.

But it wasn't her fault that they argued that day.

It wasn't her fault that his car into the ditch did sway.

He was on his way home bringing her flowers.

He'd be with her in a few more hours.

And as her love waited in heaven,
her song became his.

Faithfully, my heart remains,
Faithfully, my heart refrains,
From love, from laughter, from everything,
That's dear to me until you bring,
Your love back to me.

A few years passed with both singing the same song,
Until the angel realized
he had to make right the wrong.
Her melancholy tune made his heart sink.
So, upon a cloud he started to think.
His young bride would have a life very long.
It wasn't fair to her to be singing this song.
Because he loved her with all his heart,
He knew his true love should have a new start.
So, he wrote a new song especially for her,
A song to help mend a heart so young and pure.
Some sad songs have a happy end,

And this is how his song did begin.

You are the part of me that is the best of me.
You are the part of me that makes me feel free.
You need to let me go; I've got wings to fly.
You need to let go and give love another try.

He sang this song into her soul with a loving heart.

He sang it to his young bride so she could have a

brand-new start.

He sang it to her night and day.

And while in another's arms she'd sway.

He repeated it to her while she said I do.

He sang it because his love was true.

And as her tears of sadness turned to tears of joy,

on her wedding day.

He sang to himself quietly these words,

he couldn't say.

If you ever need me, I'll be at your side,
If you need shelter into my arms you can hide.
I'll always love you forever and a day,

In my heart your love will always stay.
Be joyous my love, that's my wish for you,
May you find happiness together
are my wishes for you two.

Take Some Time to Deal

I know that this may sound to some

a little unappealing.

But take some time to overcome

what you're dealing.

By setting aside some moments

for some healing.

To let go of the emotions

you've been concealing.

Because when you hide

your feelings instead of revealing.

From yourself and your mental health

you are only stealing.

Hidden emotions have a way

of reeling up to the minds ceiling.

Like a volcano

the pressure can leave you squealing.

So don't trap them inside

using avoidance to continue their sealing.

Helping Others Grieve

Helping someone grieve is an easy thing to do. It mostly consists of listening to them and not just talking about you. Being an active listener is harder than you think. But having these skills is how people truly link. When you speak to someone you have a choice. Do you really want to listen to them or hear your own voice? If you choose to hear them, this is lesson one. Let them just speak and speak until they are done.

Lesson two is a bit harder but worth the try. Try to truly understand what they have said to clarify. Sometimes when they hear what's said through your word. They can more easily decipher the wisdom from the absurd. Remember there are a lot of emotions intertwined in grieving. And the conversations' goal is in what the other person is receiving. Being heard and really listened to is a truly wonderful gift. You are helping to relieve their angst and stress in order to uplift.

Looking Ahead

I can look ahead to a bright future.

While the wounds to my heart I continue to suture.

Mending together that which was undone.

Creating a new me and a life just begun.

Happiness lays before me

as I work towards my goals.

Without you my life has taken on a few more roles.

I will still miss you and that is without a doubt.

But that isn't a good enough

reason to just sit and pout.

Because in my heart I realize I'm not really without.

You will be there to guide me

as I wonder what you'd do.

If you were beside me and I was listening to you.

Your presence in my life will always be there.

The bond that we had we will continue to share.

No need to live a life of despair.

For you are with me and you really do care.

Forever by Your Side

She tells the story that she was

pregnant and expecting a little guy.

That day that a train struck her car and

she did not die.

The remembers the pain left her body

and she turned cold.
She felt it was her last chance
so had to make it bold.
She pleaded with a tiny angel
as sweet as can be.
To let her live on earth and
not turn her free.

The angel pleaded with heaven
for his mom to stay.
Yes, the tiny angel was his mom,
well…anyway….

He told heaven it wasn't for his life
unlived he grieved.
It was for her because he loved her
from before he was conceived.

She said with some sadness
that the little angel could only save her life.
The two of them must

endure another strife.
The two lives
must be reduced to one.
So, the little angel told her
not to worry their bond isn't done.

Soon she'd become
pregnant again.
The little angel said it's not if
but when.
He gave his mother a hug
one last time.
He said don't worry,
Soon you'll be back in your prime.

Until then I will always
be by your side.
I know it's painful to be apart,
it's something we must abide.

She then said, he died that day
my angel flew back to heaven.

But see that boy over there
on the slide he's 7.

He is my angel, my heart, my friend,
and though he was born and forgot,
Love doesn't require proof,
It's the same little soul that I got.

As his mother I stay at his side
to guard and protect,
but while he's playing
I have time to
reflect.

Life and hearts recover too.
My child and I are an interconnected
weave of heaven's love
and so are you!

Forgiving Yourself and Others

It takes great humility and humbleness
and a loss of pride.
To acknowledge one's mistakes
when you can so easily hide.
You were given free will,
so you could truly be free.
As a test of your strength
and of your humility.
The questions I ask of you is
will you come out of your shell?
Or stay imprisoned inside
your self-created hell?
See the steps in front of you,
it's the beginning of a stair.
Come back into the light,
I offer this dare.
Rebuild the steps with forgiveness and
let acceptance be the bricks you lay.
Your tools have been given to you freely,
there is no debt to pay.
Don't get wrapped up in another's
opinions or deception,
Because you were made perfect from the inception.
Within you are the tools that will give you peace.
Forgive yourself and others
and the discourse will cease.

Sorrow Your Own Way

It matters not how you sorrow,
whether you did it yesterday
or from tomorrow borrow.
There is no principle,
no rules or time frame,
no one handles it the same.
Grief is as individual as a fingerprint.
It can be a very long haul or short stint.
It can be a learning lesson
or fiendish foe.
You may think you understand it,
then question what you know.
So, throw out all your ideas and notions,
And just experience the raw emotions.
And when it comes to others
let them express their druthers.
Everyone thinks they know what to say,
But nothing is written it's a brand-new play.
The best way to handle things is as they occur.
Because when you try to overthink thingsthey can
become a blur.

Grief has many stages and affects everyone differently.

Below is a sample guide to grief.

So Many Emotions

We have many emotions and feelings

some may seem confusing at times,

For example.

I am angry and I'm grieving.

There is a difference between the two.

But somehow we find ourselves

bridged between the two.

At times we may feel happy then suddenly cry.

Or something we love to do,

we no longer wish to try.

Grief strikes us hard in a lot of different ways,

It can feel constant,

or go away for days.

No matter where you are in this process take heart,

You are doing fine,

you're most likely not falling apart,

Death is a part of the process of birth,

It's just the cyclical rhythm on planet earth.

Death leaves a heartache no one can heal, love leaves a memory no one can steal.

IRISH HEADSTONE

I Am Not a Victim

I know that I'm not a victim,
Nor is any of this my fault.
None of this happened to me,
No reason to put my life on halt.

I am not sure when I'll be ready
to shed myself of these tears.
For some it takes a few days,
And for others it takes some years.

So please don't mistake my sorrow,
For an inability to enjoy each day.
I am in control of my emotions,
I can feel sad one minute
then go out and play.

A Better Person

Each day that passes I miss you more.

If I could turn back time to before.

Back to the days where

my best memories are.

Bringing you close to me from the afar.

But I know that you're in a peaceful place now.

So, I make to you this solemn vow.

I will make sure some of your wishes do transpire.

I will do good things for others to lift you up higher.

I have learned just how precious life can be.

And I will be a better person now because of thee.

It's Showtime

Until that last curtain call on that one sunny day.
You're on the stage and you're the play.

Billions of stars are watching as you make your
debut.
Give a good performance, by letting your goodness
shine true.

Sing if you want to sing, dance if you want to dance.
Love if you want to love, but, give yourself the
chance.

Don't worry or doubt, sit in silence or pout.
Stand up for heaven's sake and make yourself shout!

If you make a mistake, don't forget there are other
scenes.
Maybe you bombed a little in one, but in the end,
your audience will know what the play means.

If you've got stage fright, don't worry, because the worst critic is you.
After all you created the play so you're the best one to judge it too.

The stars watching are like proud parents teaching their children how to walk.
And in baby steps, encouragingly they will only talk

It doesn't really matter to them what your play is all about. If you let your inner beauty and love stream out.

And if you follow these words of advice till that last curtain call. You're guaranteed an ovation so stand proudly and tall.

Positive Actions

I am taking positive action

in all areas of my life.

I am eliminating all the things

that bring me strife.

I am going to turn my mourning

into a good morning.

I am going to turn my sorrow

into a brighter tomorrow.

I am going to take the steps

that I need to take.

I am going to do the things I should

in your name's sake.

So Sorry for Your Loss

I am so sorry for your loss

I hear them say.

Or just be thankful for the time you had,

or turn to God and pray.

Words of wisdom seemingly

coming from everywhere,

To help guide me and look

after me with love and care.

Earth Angels you could call them

whispering through a family member or friend.

Saying the things, I need to hear

and helping my mind

from the clouds to ascend.

Wonderful As You Are

You are wonderful just the way you are.

You are beautiful,

just like a shining star.

Never doubt your self-worth,

because you are worthy of love.

Never doubt anything

You were made in the image

of the goodness from above.

Be your magnificent self, be strong and true.

Be the same goodness,

that resides within you.

You are wonderful, just the way you are.

You are beautiful,

just like a shining star.

Avoiding Grief

There will be times when you may want to set aside your grief. So here are some suggestions to make it a bit less brief. Schedule some visits with family or friends. Or go to a meeting when feeling low. Distractions like these are often good ways to help make the sorrow go. And while you're meeting with others focus on them and what they need. While it may not help your situation, you will feel better when you do a good deed. For life is an exchange of ideas and thoughts. And when said in love you often give yourself the help you sought.

Acceptance is the Key

As time slowly passes me by,
And with each tear that I cry.
I think that maybe it is time.

To free myself as I've committed no crime.
I shouldn't be punishing myself so,
I am still here, I didn't go.

So, I will start to pick up my hearts broken pieces,
And like a warden open the cell that releases.
I've been a prisoner of my own desires.
Just waiting and waiting to see what transpires.
Trying in vain to hold back time.
Wasting my prime to hold on to the sublime.

= Acceptance is the Key =

Free at last I will not let time slowly pass me by,
I will make the most of life and give it my best try.
I will let go of the sadness and all the madness
and replace it with a heart full of gladness.
I will appreciate life more than ever now,
and this I make as my solemn vow.

I Cannot Always Be the Light

I realize I cannot always be the light for others

like a lamp post.

Smiling and pretending all is well

like a good host.

Sometimes I need to just let my tears flow.

Releasing my sorrow, letting it all go.

Even the sun sometimes hides behind the cloud,

It's okay to protect myself and in comfort enshroud.

And when the last tear drops fall,

I will better be able to stand braver and tall.

Please Stay with Me My Angel

Please stay with me my angel…

Help somebody, is anybody there?

Please stay with me my angel…

Help us someone? Does anybody care?

Please stay with me my angel…

Honey I see a light in the distance.

Please stay with me my angel…

The light is getting nearer maybe its assistance.

Please stay with me my angel…

I think I see someone in the light.

Please stay with me my angel…

I think it's a guardian angel bright.

Please stay with me my angel…

He says he's called for an ambulance.

Please stay with me my angel…

Honey, he says he's a doctor, we have a chance!

Please stay with me my angel…

He missed the turn, and our accident he did see.

Please stay with me my angel…

He saw our car wedged into the tree.

Please stay with me my angel…

Can you hear the siren in the distance dear?

Please stay with me my angel…

Can you see the white light it's so near?

Please stay with me my angel…,

Honey the pressure on my chest hurts so much.

Please stay with me my angel…

I think someone's pounding, it's not a light touch.

Please stay with me my angel…

Can you see the beautiful lady in the light?

Please stay with me my angel…

She wants me to walk away into the bright.

Please stay with me my angel…

But I can't leave you honey, not now.

Please stay with me my angel…

I'll never leave you this I vow.

Please stay with me my angel…

She left but another's coming forward.

Please stay with me my angel…

He keeps saying….

Please stay with me my angel…

His voice sounds just like yours…

Oh yes, yes, I will stay with you, my angel.

Please stay with me my angel…

Honey I can't move forward I'm trapped.

"What's the situation doctor?" asked the arriving paramedic. The Dr. stated "The gentleman died on impact. I did CPR on the woman for 10 minutes.

There is a faint pulse, and she's still unconscious. She has broken bones and lacerations on her head. Her neck injuries will likely result in her being paralyzed. If she has the will to live, she should pull through. Put her in the ambulance.

Grief and It's Cousins

The family of grief is a large and perilous one There are many cousins and none of them fun. There is sorrow, misery and sadness that leaves you blue, Anguish, pain, distress and affliction too.

There's suffering and a heartache that is very deep also. And desolation, despondency, dejection and woe. Despair, angst, lament, remorse, regret and mourning. And now that your aware of most of them please heed this warning.

Though all may seem too heavy a burden to bear. They are simply temporary emotions, and you can transcend them if you dare. There are a few magic tools that will help you get by. They are acceptance, forgiveness, hope and faith, give them a try.

A Life Unborn

And the mom sadly said…

A life taken from inside the womb

A life taken and casually entombed.

A forgotten angel without a chance

A forgotten angel without a dance

I am so sorry little angel for the life you'll never live.

I am so sorry for the love I couldn't give.

I still believe in my right to choose.

But why can't I stop thinking of the baby I did lose?

I'll mark this day on my calendar,

As a painful reminder of the grief, I must endure.

And the little angel sadly said…

Mom I can see the pain that your feeling,

Mom beside you I am kneeling.

I know exactly why you made the choices you did.

But, mom, I didn't die, I'm a little kid.

Your guardian angel whisked me away,

And God made me older in a single day.

You did what you thought should be done.

Ending a life that had not yet begone.

You believed you saved me from a major birth
defect.

And now you are feeling lonely as you reflect.

Just know that I love you just the same.

As I'd have loved you if I were born deaf, blind and
lame.

And the mom cried…

Not realizing the little angel was by her side.

No Reason or Rhyme

Sometimes there is just

no reason or rhyme,

And I need to retreat

and just give myself time.

To be like a tree

as the winds around me may swirl,

With branches that bend

as the debris around me twirl.

And when the storm eventually

passes me by,

I will be stronger than ever

and able to try,

To try my best

to follow my path.

Stronger than ever

to withstand any wrath.

Lean on Them

It's okay to lean on your family and friends. That's part of what they are there for in the end. They know you better than most. They are there to tell your problems too and of successes boast. Just try not to overburden them with too many cares, you need to balance things out by also listening to theirs.

If you can't find a family member or friend in which to confide. Find someone else who you look up to who had someone close to them that died. They can help you through your grieving, give you support and guide.

Fairy Princess Angel

Softly on angel wings in the still of the night,

arrived at a home, a small angel, shiny and bright.

She had fairy glow skin, and her eyes wide as a doe

she glided up the staircase wondering which way to
go.

When suddenly appeared a small child, who grabbed
her by the hand.
She looked up at her and tried to understand.

The child's mind was full of curiosity, she wanted to
know,
"Are you a fairy princess? please say it's so!"

The angel said sweetly I'm like a fairy Godmother,
but I watch over you while you sleep.
So, you better go back to bed now, and not make a
peep.

"Huh?" Said the little girl in confusion.
"I thought that was the job of the sandman?"
She wasn't quite buying the angels delusion.

She then added "are you sure you're a fairy
godmother because you look more like the Tooth
Fairy to me.
I have a picture of her in a book, do you want to
see?"

The little angel didn't know what to say or do.
She was not supposed to ever be seen, so quickly
out the window she flew.

The next morning at breakfast the little girl shared the
story with her brother and dad.
She said, "My fairy godmother came to the house
last night, I think I made her mad.

Her dad looked at her and said, "can you pass me
the pancake, the big one beneath".
She replied, "I told her she looked like the tooth fairy
cause her skin was as white as teeth."

Her brother looked at her and said, "pass the syrup",
In a voice that was much louder, she he said, "She
had sparkly stuff all over her. Maybe she stole the
sandman's powder."

So, no one listened to the child that day,
She herself soon forgot as she went out to play.

YOU MATTER

To be

fully alive

It's no trivial affair

From it you cannot tear

You occupy time and space

And from this you cannot erase

Your life does matter on every level

And from existence you cannot dishevel

You remain fixed in a logical order and pattern

And the positive, negative, yin and yang

Are essentials from which you sprang

These particles will never scatter

They're substance and matter

Not only are you matter

You really do matter

You are whole

You are

Soul

From Beginning to End

The circle of life from beginning to end,

Is a never-ending process

in which we all blend.

No matter your religion, race or creed,

The termination of life is in our deed.

So, knowing that your time on earth will expire,

Enjoy each moment and fulfill your desire.

And if you come across someone

who's lost hope,

Remind them of how precious life is

to help them cope.

Enjoy this gift you've been given since birth.

Make the most of your stay

here on planet earth.

Sometimes I Don't Feel Tough

I admit not having you in my life often feels so rough

And sometimes I feel I just am not tough enough.

To deal with the grief that I feel inside.

When it would be so easy to just run away and hide.

So, I try and feed myself with hope and faith.

And listen to what others around me saith.

I hold on to the memories to hold on to you.

I tell myself I'm strong, what else can I do?

No matter what I do I don't feel tough.

Is there something I'm missing am I not doing enough?

And she saw the note she had placed for herself

a few days earlier and felt peace. The note said…

Relax, you are doing great,

You just have a lot now on your plate.

Things will get better you will see.

Just have a little faith and just let it be.

Sometimes it's just better to let go and trust.

That everything will work out as it must.

Be kind to yourself for what you're going through.

Write notes to yourself, etc., if you need to.

You Are the Architect

You are the architect of your life; you have the power to lessen your greatest strife. Within you is the ability to move from a place of sadness, to leave the madness and enter a place of acceptance and gladness. You can start anew each day and in peace and happiness stay. Because you are truly magnificent and a blessing to others when you dare, just by keeping your heart open and focusing on others who need care. Everybody experiences a great loss and pain, it's part of life and engrained in the terrain. But just as life has peaks and valleys low.

You remain strong and with each obstacle you grow.
You know how to take life's difficulties one by one,
And handle things with grace in the light of the sun.

A Love that Surpasses Time

Golden strands of curls,

Framed the faces of the pretty girls.

Golden strands woven into armor,

Framed the body of their charmer.

But when he gazed upon her face,

A flood of memories came back that he couldn't

erase.

Such fair ladies he said as his eyes met upon his

sun.

The startled ladies backed away, all but one.

Not her, she stared right through his piercing gaze.

The more she looked the more her world turned to

haze.

Her mind told her to leave, but her heart begged her

to stay.

Hypnotized in his eyes, her body began to sway.

Before she could fall to the ground, he took her in his

embrace.

She looked up at him and began to remember his face.

Her smile and her eyes revealed their love story.

She remembered their past life and remembered all its glory.

As the angel released his grip and she stood upon her own two feet.

She knew that in the future they both would again meet.

He flew away in an instant as one of the girls began to scream.

Then his love fainted to the ground but awoke with a beautiful dream.

He was so happy to have found her, he wondered where she'd went.

Now that he found her, he would watch over her, until her last day on earth was spent.

Death Cannot Break the Bond

I realize that death
does not break the bond we shared.
And the absence of your presence
doesn't mean you never cared.
All is still as it once was in my heart.
And from the memories of you I will not depart.
I will treasure every moment up to the last.

Carrying you with me
rather than leaving you in the past.

In Grief They Said

All we really have is that which we are,

A flesh body and a shiny soul bright as a star.

We can let our light shine far and wide,

Or dim it as away we hide.

Everything else really doesn't matter,

It's a distraction, and endless chatter.

So let us choose to be bright as the sun,

to encourage and love everyone.

Until this life is someday undone.

Let us appreciate it and have some fun.

Passing the Baton

Imagine there is no death,
Just a passing of a baton.
And that we are all on the same team,
From dusk to dawn.
Just because the first runner
is no longer in view,
Their value and worth
are still just as true.
It's easy to stop and mourn
that which we do not understand.
Or feel as if it's our own lives
that we've lost command.
So we need to remember
we are also in this race.
And there is no glory in quitting,
So we need to step up the pace.

May Love Lift You Up

In this time of sadness and sorrow,

wondering what will happen in the world tomorrow,

I say this prayer to help the healing start,

to bring calmness and peace to your heart.

Let love lift you up from worried dreams,

Carrying you from the dark into moon beams.

Watching over you until the sun streams.

Until the sparkle in your eye's again gleams.

Let love lift you up with angel wings.

High enough so your heart sings.

High enough to feel the love in everything.

High enough to see all the good life brings.

Through each day forward may you gently glide.

Safe and secure with love by your side.

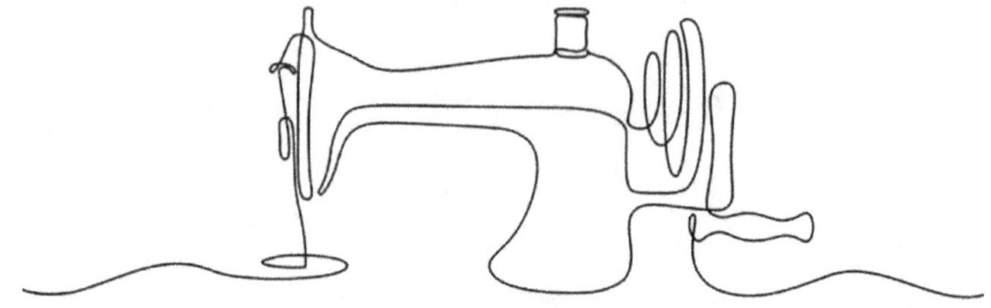

The Fabric of Life

Some paths are shiny and lit with gold.
Some are weathered, dirty and old.

Some will lead to hearts desires.
Others towards thieves and liars.

It's your choice where you want to go.
So, the angels must constantly sew.

Loving angels carry a needle and thread,
To stitch around the paths, we tread.

A stitch for time, a stitch for hope,
A stitch for love, a stitch to cope.

So many stitches around our path,
Because we unweave our own wrath.

Scattered thoughts and scattered dreams.
Angels mending at the seams.

Straight stitch, overcast stitch, zigzag stitch and
embroider.
The angels stitch along our paths, custom made to
order.

Stitch by stitch and one by one.
Part of a beautiful, patterned fabric that can't be
undone.

Intertwining, interlacing, interloping, interceding the
fabric of life goes around us
and through us connects us and directs us.

A common thread without beginning or end that
binds and unites, stretches and tightens as it links us
to our future and past. Thus, you'd be wise to make
your stitches last.

Mend and strengthen your own fragile thread,
Carefully choosing the paths that you tread.

Love Completely

Love yourself completely.

Treat yourself ever so sweetly.

Hug your inner child today.

Allow yourself to rest and play.

You have been through a lot.

The toughest of life's lessons you've been taught.

You've endured the trials and tribulations of loss.

And in the waves of emotions, you did toss.

So, climb into the lifeboat and come ashore.

Warm yourself in the sun and feel joy once more.

Times Trying and Hard

Though these times may be trying and hard,

And even small things seem to cut

like a glass shard,

You have the tools

within you to ease the pain,

To heal your heart

and quiet your brain.

You are stronger than you think you are,

You know when to fight

or steer from your troubles afar.

Tiny Shiny Orb

I heard in the news today

about the tiny shiny orb

A few people saw it but for most

it was hard to absorb

The ones that did not believe,

said that upon it their own eyes must stare

Yet, I thought it's kind of ironic

because they themselves can't see the air

Humans were designed to only see

and hear certain things

It's a lesson in faith and of the good things it brings

Blessed are those who are able

to see with childlike eyes

For they are innocent and pure enough

to not need to ask all the whys

When you analyze everything

the mysteries disappear

And you may lose the ability to see things

like the tiny shiny sphere

Grief Reminds Us We Are Alive

Grief reminds us that we are alive. It's a coping mechanism that helps us thrive. The sorrow that we feel and the pain, reminds us not to live our life in vain. It can show us that our heart still cares. And warn us that we better take care of our affairs. If we take the time, we can learn things from grief. It can make us change, turn over a new leaf. It can help us see clearly things once unseen. It can make us appreciate even a mundane routine. For when are forced to take a glimpse towards deaths door. We often realize the importance of life a lot more.

Never Give up the Hope

Never give up the hope

that better things are coming,

And never give up faith

as it will keep your soul humming.

Look ahead towards the rainbows

that follow the clouds,

Turn away from any negativity

that enshrouds.

Brighter days are coming,

they will soon be here.

You'll be able to care more deeply

for all that you hold dear.

Thankful for the Time

I am thankful for your time spent with me.

I am thankful for your love eternally.

I am thankful for the memories we shared.

I am thankful because I know that you truly cared.

And although I feel the pain of your leaving,

To you I will still be cleaving,

I can live my life happily and true,

While celebrating the time I had with you.

Wings of Love

Grief gave me wings in which to spread love.
Understanding the pain
I can be more like a peace dove.

I can comfort others better who are in need.
There's so much suffering in the world indeed.

And with my wings I gained some hope.
I understand now the sorrow
and can better help others to cope.

With an eagles view I can show others
all the beauty around.
I can share with others
how purpose and meaning can still be found.
There's a lot I can do
while still living on the ground.

The Pain Will Heal

The pain in your heart will heal.

Now say it out loud with some zeal.

Truer words were never spoken.

Because a heart really cannot be broken.

It can "feel" crushed, and torn

It can "feel" forsaken and forlorn

But I say this without a doubt.

You are alive and your heart is too.

Feelings of happiness will replace the blue.

The pain in your heart will heal.

And though it may seem surreal.

You will grow stronger through this ordeal.

Just give yourself time to mend.

And never forget to be your own best friend.

A World Full of Chances
=.

Without chances life would cease to exist,

Without chances the mystery would have no twist.

Nothing would change and the whole world would fall
apart,

But how does one attract a chance, to make a brand-
new start.

Before one can take a chance, the mind must surely
learn to see it,

For sometimes chances pass right by because the
untrained mind deems them unfit.

Even deeper still where do these chance random
events of chaos come from?

These tiny little miracles that can cause massive
chain reactions from a tiny crumb.

Can chaos exist in a universe based on patterns and order?
Or is it the molecule that makes order from disorder?

Can everything come out of nothing that was before?
Or could it be that our universe has an opening and heaven is the door?

If we lived our lives in a petri dish,
Would chances be the variables added to our lives with a swish?

Count Your Blessings

If you focus on your blessings

and learn to count them too.

It will be easier for you to see them

and the impact on your life they can do.

They can guide you on your journey

and during difficult times help you through.

So, practice counting your blessings

one by one.

Why look down towards despair

when you can look up towards the sun?

Together No Matter What

Girl: Will you love me, during the good and bad?

Will you love me, when I make you mad?

Boy: You are my angel, my destiny so true.

You are my angel, God blessed me with you.

Will you love me, if my hair turns gray?

Will you love me, if I sat all day?

Girl: You are my angel; my heart is now content.

You are my angel; you are heaven sent.

Will you love me, with wrinkled skin?

Will you love me, no matter what shape I'm in?

Boy: You are my angel, for you my heart beats.

You are my angel, for you my smile greets.

Will you love me, if I gain too much weight?

Girl: You are my angel, there is no debate.

Boy: You are my angel, my soul mate.

The Gentle Rain

How I yearn for your embrace

I would love to hold you just one more time

But you are quiet as a mime

Whisked away in your prime

Leaving me here all alone

Taking the greatest love, I had ever known

Oh why, oh why, I moan

Our love should have only grown

Not cut down like a tree

Abruptly reducing us to a me

And the angel sent a gentle rain

to wash away the pain

to help remove the tear stain

Upon her face

And leave some peace in its place.

And placed a rainbow close in view,

To help restore and renew,

A saddened soul still in grief,

A tattered heart needing relief.

Wings Unbound

Heaven is home to creatures on high,
The angels who play and longingly sigh.
Remembering lives long ago lived,
Remembering love long ago gived.
Through tears of happiness
and mournful regret,
An angel is one whom will never forget.
The love they found upon the ground,
Is carried to heaven on wings unbound.

Some People Give Love

Some people give love and demand it in return.

Some people collect love, even from those whom they show no concern.

Some people crave love so deeply it hurts them from within.

The need for love becomes like a cancer, devouring and overpowering, in a self-inflicted battle they most likely won't win.

Some people build walls around their heart so hard Cupids sharpest arrow could not penetrate.

Their reasoning though rational is not even left open for debate.

Some prefer living life alone.

Perhaps feeling unworthy, as if for something they need to atone.

For me, I learned to rely on myself, and really, there's been little strife.

I tend to run away from love given, but all in all I've created a happy life.

I have very few regrets that the love birds for me
rarely did sing,

I can still give my love to others; in the good deeds I
can bring.

Each of us is a tiny speck of this rainbow of love.

Different hues and shades of colors none below or
above.

None of us is perfect, we are just trying to cope.

We fill our minds with nonsense, but our hearts are
still filled with hope.

There is no narrow construct to define love and its
wonderful power,

with magic so beautiful it lifts souls as high as a
tower.

There is no right or wrong, there's really nothing to
say or do,

If love seems to escape you, you need only to see
through.

See through your own darkness, clear the clutter
from your mind,

From life's troubles, you really need to hit the rewind.

Imagine you're a child and everything is fresh and
new.

Forget the shoulds and woulds and to thine own self
be true.

Love is everywhere, you simply need to see it.

Love is everywhere, you simply need to be it.

Don't judge love or try and make it something that it's
not.

For when you start to doubt it, you will lose what you
have sought.

The Promised Land

Said the women to the angel.

They say that a seed of faith shall bring,

Wonders, miracles and everything.

But, the seed of faith is not a part,

Of the cavernous pit I call my heart.

Where it once was a well overflowing,

When my inner child was glowing,

Reality reared its ugly head,

I fear that now my heart is dead.

Decades of tangled memories fill my mind,

Try as I might I could not unbind,

My dreams and aspirations,

From the burdens of my life's station.

The things I wished to do, couldn't be done,

I couldn't trade my security for a little fun.

So, through the years the soil I turned

And the butter I churned.

I worked the farm dawn to dusk

The weeds I'd pull, the corn I'd husk.

Till my face was weathered with lines,

And my broken body that this wheelchair confines.

Yes, I'm weathered, beaten and old,

And, I've got nothing left to hold,

The land I cared for has been sold,

A lifetime of work traded for some gold.

Then she looked at me and laughed,

I guess life really gave me the shaft.

I could hear the spunk in her voice,

I felt the inner anguish of her choice.

So, I just touched her on her forehead,

And smiled as I said…

There is little use in lamenting about the past,

And worrying about things that cannot last.

I said it was a noble thing she did,

And I considered her life to be splendid.

Had she not chosen to care for the fields,

The thing of beauty her life yields.

Leaving the burden of her life's station,

Would not have led to any more elation.

I then looked into an alternate reality and said.

Not only would your life have been less worth living,

Many suffered without what you were giving.

I explained to her.

Each crop brought blessings and peace.

The more you gave the more the release.

Life is about doing what's right and good.

Not just doing what you want, but what you should.

I shared with her about the gentleman who pulled

over to gaze at her farm.

It caused him to miss a traffic accident that would

have caused great harm.

And the single mom with cancer and barely enough

to eat,

who used to stop by the stand for fresh vegetables to

eat,

and how it was through nutrition that her cancer was

beat.

On and on I read to her from a list that was so long it

reached out the hospital door.

I guess I put her to sleep because she began to

snore.

When suddenly out of the corner of my eye I did see,

My friend the angel of death looking at me.

He gave me a look and I instantly knew,

That my job as her guardian angel would soon be
through.

Her eyes remained still and shut as she woke and
took my hand.
Her body laid peaceful and still as I took her to the
promised land.

When we arrived, she looked around,
at the beauty that abounds
and with a great smile said,
"Do you have any jobs here working on a farm?"
She said it with a new sense of peace and a youthful
charm.

You Are Creativity

You are creativity.

Manifested by your positivity.

Wherever your path may lead.

You are both the planter and the seed.

Let the fruit of your life give nourishment to all,

Winter, spring, summer and fall.

You are also the gardener responsible for the

direction you grow,

Whether it be high, low, hither or fro.

Let your life nourish the soil,

For future gardeners who choose to toil,

Planting their seeds with care,

In the garden of life that we all share.

Intent On Screening

There are some intent on screening.

Another's true intent and meaning.

They often judge the things another does,

Yet they don't ask why or care

about the because.

They are the jury and the judge too.

And, no matter what you say or do,

There is no pleasing a person with an inflexible mind.

No need to hurl insults back or be unkind.

Just give them their space and back far away.

You've got enough on your plate,

save them for a rainy day.

You Have Emotional Intelligence

You have the ability to recognize your own feelings.

You can discern and use your different emotions in

order to help in your dealings. You use the

information to help guide your thinking behavior. And

you can adjust your emotions to your needs at your

favor. You are not a victim of your emotions you control them. You are the master of your emotions and from within you they stem. You have emotional intelligence its true. So, use as you need it controlling your emotions and not letting them control you.

Forever in My Heart

Forever in my heart,

And in my thoughts too.

You will live on,

As a part of me that's true.

You will always be my friend,

From now until the end.

Forever in my heart.
As I make my new start.
And on the planet live on,
As a part of this world with oceans blue.
I will enjoy life again,
Mindful of where I have been.

And I will celebrate each day,
And count my blessings along the way.
For you are forever in my heart.

TAKE CARE OF YOURSELF

He searched his heart for the right words to say,

as he was about to leave her at college to stay.

So, he grabbed a pen and wrote a quick note,

of the things he hoped his daughter would devote.

He said…

Use each lesson learned to sharpen your mind,

feed it with introspection and direction.

Take care of your heart,

feed it with love and affection.

Take care of your body,

feed it with healthy foods packed with nutrition.

And exercise to ward off natural attrition.

Take care of your soul,

feed it with faith and hope.

If you do these things,

with most obstacles you will cope.

She found the note in her suitcase and replied with a

text…

I love you dad with all my heart,

I will treasure your note as I make my brand-new

start.

The moral to this story is simple and true,

It's something we all need to work on and do.

Choose your words wisely and keep them positive.

They are lessons to be learned and gifts to give.

If you focus on the worries and the chatter,

Another's soul you'll probably only batter.

Searching for Signs

If you're lacking purpose or direction, you can make

life more meaningful and fun by searching for signs.

Believing in signs that serve to guide and protect you

can be divine. You simply need to open your mind and your heart to believe it. Then search for the signs to help you achieve it. The signs could be the direction the birds suddenly fly in the air. The signs could be the way the wind is blowing through your hair. If you open your heart to the world of possibilities, and your mind to inspiration and creativity, and then relax and just let it be, even if your eyes are shut you can see. Because the best way is not always the easiest way to go follow the signs and they will help you know. Instead of wandering aimlessly to and fro.

Fear Not

And the angel said…

Fear not, I am a mere angel fallen from the sky.

Tear not, its good news that I have, and I'll tell you why.

I traded my wings and my halo of gold,

to come here and tell you a story, ancient and old.

It's a story about an angel just like me,

and a fair maiden such as thee.

Much like you her eyes were full of stars and hope.

Much like you her only ambition was to climb the rope.

She wanted to be someday as high as God.

The kind of person that others would want to emulate and applaud.

That's when this handsome and very helpful angel

stepped in.

And how her mortal life would soon begin.

Now if you're interested, I'll tell you more.

If you're not, I'll just turn and walk out that door.

And the girl said…

No, please stay, I want to hear everything!

I want to hear about the gifts the angel did bring.

Did she become rich and gain fame?

And for me could you do the same?

And the Angel said…

Well, she gave up a garden and gained a world.

Not a bad priced as her life unfurled.

Where she was once bare,

she now gained clothes.

To cover herself from her head down to her toes.

But before I go on with my tale,

I notice that you're looking a little pale.
It's past lunch and I know what ails.

I just happen to have here a beautiful apple won't
you take a bite.
I promise you that it will bring you great delight!

In fact, some might say that each bite is full of glory.
Yes, take a bite, as I continue my story.

Her guardian angel who had been sitting on her other
shoulder,
Spoke a bit louder and with a voice that was much
bolder.

All that glitters is not gold,
Listen not to this angel who has fallen from the fold.

The richness you desire you have already attained,
Bite not of this apple for its juice will leave you
stained.

A mark upon you that will attract life's worse kind,
People who'll deceive you and attack you from
behind.

Wealth is not all it's cracked up to be,
Often it becomes the prison of a soul longing to be
free.

It can still your voice
and leave you without choice,
And instill fear,
deep within your ear,
till negativity is all you can hear.

The only wealth worth a grain of salt is that earned
by doing good.
Ill-gotten gains come at a high price,
Don't throw your life away at the toss of a dice.

Asking for Forgiveness

I am sorry for some things and ask forgiveness now.

I need to apologize for some stuff that I did allow.

First, I am sorry for the things left unsaid or undone.

I should have done more to fix things instead of

having fun.

I am sorry for the arguments and misunderstandings.

Usually started on baseless standings.

And if you were here today you could have your way a lot.

Some things are way better just left forgot.

Funny how the small things seemed so big when you were here.

And now that you are gone, they seem so much less severe.

I have learned a lesson from this that's for sure.

Never take anyone for granted as life can end premature.

And forgiveness will not change the past,

But it can bring positive change to the future fast.

Be Your Best

You've been given a small crumb
And it's up to you to multiply its sum

The more you give, the more will come your way
Love's dividends are returned to you every day

Those who know what I'm talking about
Have never really been without

They're work has already begun
They are the ones who are bringing out the sun

If you can't find what you need to give
Then you really can't truly live

It was placed in your heart and it's a feeling
It's a commodity for anything in which your dealing

It's the best part of you that you can give away
When you're dealing in love
the sun is shining every day.

A Life Without

One by one the days roll by.

Two by two the nights ask why.

Where are you, she cries out!

Why am I living a life without?

Too soon you were taken from my embrace,

Now I pray, I won't forget your face.

Three by three the weeks roll by.

Four by four the months ask why.

Where are you, she cries out!

Why am I here living a life without?

I used to feel your presence next to me,

Now I feel emptiness where you used to be.

Five by five the years roll by.

Six by six the decades ask why.

Where are you, she cries out!

Why am I here living a life without?

The angels that took you away,

Deserted me, so here alone I stay,

Seven by seven opens the heavens.

Eight by eight she's shown the gate.

Where are you, her soul cries out?

Why am I here living a life without?

A voice replies, loving and true.

Open your eyes, I've always been beside you.

Nine by Nine her divine life is fine.

= but =

Ten by Ten

They decide to live on earth again.

Comfort of an Angel

Snap bang went the thunder,

Down poured the rain.

Finding no goodness,

The little angel was in pain.

Moaning and groaning,

Upon the street she laid.

Dying from lack of kindness,

Her life might slowly fade.

The chilly frost began to take its toll.

It nipped at her ferociously,

Battered her poor soul.

She tried in vain,

To spread her wings to fly,

But they were frozen solid,

She feared that she would die.

Nobody took notice,

Of me she did sigh.

As she lay on the concrete,

The frost on her gave her form.

Out of the corner of her eye,

A beggar saw this tiny angel in the storm.

She thought it was a hallucination,

she had to blink twice.

But to her surprise, the angel said,

"Can you spare a grain of nice."

This tiny angel small as a pigeon,

laid down upon the street.

Begging for warmth,

and a morsel to eat.

So, the homeless lady shared her last crumb

with the angel humbly.

And she took off her coat

and wrapped it around the angel tenderly.

She sat through the cold winter's night

Sheltering her own angel in her coat.

By morning's light,

the two flew off to a place

beautiful and remote.

A New Life

An angel knelt by the bed

To cry for the living and the dead

A tired and weary mother wept

A lifeless infant by her side she kept

The angel kissed the newborn softly

Then blew her breath upon its face gently

She tried so hard to turn the baby from pale

But all her efforts would only fail

She heard the mother's cries many times before

A new life would enter then leave through the door

And while the angel knew a soul could never die

The anguish of this mother really caught her eye

So, she gave up everything and her ability to fly

She entered the infant's body and let out a cry

The pain was unbearable, her soul became fused

The body's cells latched on as a battery used

The infants brain fired up and erased knowledge past

But it was worth it for this mother had her baby at last

Lessons to Teach and Reach

I am looking for the lesson this situation

must teach me.

I am looking for the reasons

and hoping they someday reach me.

Why did I have to experience this loss at this time?

I ask questions like this

and wait for an angel to chime.

Why oh why must everything living always die?

Why oh why I wonder things like this as I cry.

And in her mourning came an answer clear.

From a familiar voice, one she held dear.

Birth and death are the circle of life.

Rejoicing on the arrival

and grieving at their death,

is a reminder of the goodness

and in the time with which you've been blessed.

Never take a thing for granted because it can be lost.

Use your time wisely for it comes at a great cost.

Welcome Home Angel

And the mother said…

I waited 9 months for my love to arrive,

anticipating the joy, they'd bring.

A gift from above to make my heart sing,

my child, my heart, my everything.

And the child thought…

Softly on the angel wings,

I arrived without anything.

A gift from above that makes my heart sing,

My family, my heart, my everything.

You Set Me Free

No matter how much I am in pain

By my side you remain

When I'm feeling down

In my sorrows drown

You give me hope

Make things easier to cope

In return for my troubles

My enjoyment doubles

You are gone but with me too.

You help keep me from feeling blue.

Full of Hope and Faith

I am full of hope and faith

that the dark clouds will pass.

I can already see the rainbows amass.

There is so much beauty everywhere.

Things that I'm appreciating now

I once barely noticed there.

Life is so fragile I have learned.

Yet I've spent a lot of it denying

the things for which I have yearned.

I have been doing the things

I thought which should be done.

When I could have been chasing rainbows

and just having more fun.

Life is priceless, our greatest wealth,

So, enjoy each and focus on your health.

As Time Passes

A long time has passed,

without you by my side.

A long time has passed,

since you were my bride.

I could have remarried

several times over the years.

But it's hard to be happy

when you're fighting back the tears.

Maybe someday

when I'm ready will I try again.

Maybe someday

when my heart has healed

a new life I'll begin.

A long time has passed,

here on the other side.

A long time has passed,

since I was your bride.

I have watched over you

throughout the years.

I've tried to bring you joy

and wipe away your tears.

Throughout your life,

no matter where you've been,

I've been there for you

then and when.

As the old man closed his eyes

and breathed his last breath.

He felt a hand upon his

leading him past death.

Through a dark tunnel he

floated without a care.

With eyes shut until

he reached her there.

He recognized her at once

 his beautiful bride.

And together they walked off,

side by side.

Mom You're with Me

Mommy, why are you sleeping in that box too high for me to see?

Won't you wake up and please play with me?

Mommy why is daddy crying so?

Why do we have to leave you here and go?

Mommy it's my birthday and I wished that you were here.

Mommy it's my first day of school and I'm full of fear.

Mommy dad lost his job, and the landlord wants the rent.

Daddy told him that on all the bills, the monies already been spent.

Mom we are living in a car now, I'm hungry and I'm cold.

Dad said it's temporary and that I should just be bold.

Mom we have an apartment, and I met a cute guy named Will.

Dad say's I'm too young to date, but I'm 14 now I'm not a kid still.

Mom I graduated from high school today and got a scholarship.

I'm going off to college soon and packing for my trip.

Mom, I'm pregnant, and not sure what I should do?

Michael says we should marry, but I don't love him so I'm blue.

Mom I had the baby she's so precious and I gave her your name.

Mom today I am marrying Michael, yeah, I know I said he's lame.

But he is such a good father, and, I have fallen in love all the same.

Mom, our little girl is in high school now, my how time does fly.

It seems like yesterday she was a baby, and soon she'll say goodbye.

Mom I just came from the doctor, the cancer has spread.

The chemo isn't working, in a few months I could be dead.

Mom, I made it, I am now in remission, yes, cancer free.

Mom thanks for always being by my side, helping me.

With Every Breath I Inhale

With every breath I inhale happiness and gladness.

With every breath I exhale my sorrow and sadness.

So, I breathe deeply and steadily and strong.

Breathing to live, breathing in a rhythmic song.

And with each breath of life I take,

The less it seems that my heart does ache.

As the oxygen feeds my cells and brings me health.

I can see more clearly my inner wealth.

I am strong right down to my inner core.

I am stronger than I ever was before.

How Much Does It Cost?

How much does it cost?

To gaze upon the stars in the sky.

How much does it cost?

To listen to birds singing.

How much does it cost?

To feel the sun upon your face.

How much does it cost?

To chase a rainbow across a meadow.

How much does it cost?

To watch a glorious sunset.

How much does it cost?

To hear the ocean crash upon the shore.

How much does it cost?

To take a walk along a peaceful path.

How much does it cost?

To listen to the laughs of children.

How much does it cost?

To swing in a swing.

How much does it cost?

To relax and watch the clouds pass by.

How much does it cost?

To dance in the rain.

How much does it cost?

To chase the fireflies.

How much does it cost?

To watch a kite fly in the park.

Injustice No More

I release my feeling of injustice.

And feelings that life is

not fair.

For I am not the only person

to have lost.

I am not the only one to have paid

this high cost.

Everyone in the world

experiences loss equally.

It's something that we can't avoid or flee.

So no longer will I feel that life's unfair.

I am choosing to open my heart and care.

Present in the Moment

I am fully present in this moment,

I am right where I need to be.

No need to have any thoughts,

I am choosing to just be peacefully.

The quiet solitude in my mind

is what I need right now.

A chance to take a breath

and recharge myself I allow.

There is really nothing more important now

than just being.

There is nothing more important now

than my own well being

A New Day

When the new day has begun,
And you can no longer see me,
Don't think our love is done,
By your side I will still be.

When the night does arrive,
And without me you are lonely,
Just because I'm not alive,
Doesn't mean you're not my only,

I'm so sorry for the pain I caused,
For leaving you alone my dear,
But you can hear my whisper in the trees,
And in the rain feel my tear.

Please don't be sad for me,
Because that really breaks my heart.
Cause I know someday you'll see,
It's just a temporary part.

When the new night has begun,
And in the darkness, you can't see me,
Just remember the setting sun,
Also, set's the night free.

Through darkness there is light,

And it brings so many treasures.
A glowing moon shines bright.
Billions of stars, too many to measure.

And when the night begins to pale,
The dawn will bring a beautiful new day.
As thoughts of me start to sail
Please know that it is okay.

And, I truly understand,
If you want to fill the empty space.
And to take another's hand.
Because I'm in a good place.

The main sadness that I feel,
Is your emptiness inside,
For I know that love is the only thing real,
And your heart should be your guide.

let your
light
Shine

Write a New Chapter

Losing someone you love is one of the saddest things to endure. But you have it in you now to focus on the one thing that is sure. Life is still full of blessings and good things and that is certain. And losing someone doesn't mean you have to close the curtain. You can keep close to your love and celebrate both your life and theirs. You can still talk to them in your prayers, while your heart repairs. Think of this loss as the beginning of a new chapter you can write. It could be full of adventure, faith, love or anything else that brings delight. Write it as a way for you to find what matters most to you, things you'd like to explore. because there is so much you can still do

EXTRA CONTENT

About Grief

Grief is the response to a loss of someone who has passed on. It's a loss of someone whom you most likely shared a bond with who's now gone. And while it commonly causes emotional reactions, it can manifest in other ways as it multiplies and fractions.

You can experience grief in your body, it can also be physical. Grief can affect your moods and cause changes that are behavioral. When it affects your thinking, it is said to be cognitive and makes you question what is true. It can also affect you culturally, spiritually, and philosophically too.

While grieving can take on any form, the following 7 stages usually are the norm. They are disbelief, denial, bargaining, anger, depression and guilt. Acceptance comes at the end and together that's how the stages are built. The symptoms of grief can be very diverse, none any better, none any worse.

Each can cause conflicts within you, these conflicts can be physical, emotional, social and religious too.

There are many ways that people feel when grief sets in. First it may come as shock and disbelief of what has just been. It can be hard to accept what happened and you may feel numb or deny it. Because when someone you love has died your feelings don't quit and your mind seeks to defy it.

A profound sadness is perhaps one of the most common symptoms of grief. Feelings of emptiness, despair, loneliness, and depression that challenge your core belief. You may feel guilty about the things you did not do or things you did not say, Or, about the feelings you're having or the thoughts and actions that you display. And, even if the loss was nobody's fault you still may feel angry and resentful. You might blame someone or feel an injustice even if the death was uneventful. Grief can also manifest itself in fear because you have experienced a significant loss. You may feel anxious, helpless or insecure and at night in the bed you may toss.

There is no magic formula to predict when the grieving will end. Grieving is a highly individual experience and on many factors it will depend. These factors could include everything from your personality type to your coping style, your life experiences, faith, how close the attachment are, are also on the aisle. So do not rush grief, just let it runs its course. And do not rush others who grieve it will only lead to remorse.

While there are lots of tools and tricks to help grief go away. There will most likely always be a little that will stay. When we lose someone that we can't get back, you may want to retreat from others and going into your shell but having the support of others is vital and helps unlock the cell. It's important to express the pain and loss because it is a lot to carry. Seeking help from many sources is best as you will find everyone's suggestions will vary.

Try to seek out those people who care about you the most. Or look for groups that offer support or perhaps you could start one and host. Support groups are great for helping you deal with what you're going through. Sometimes some expert advice helps when you don't have a clue. When you listen to what others are going through it can make you feel less alone. Especially when you hear stories that are like your own.

Remember that many people feel awkward when trying to comfort someone in grieving. Grief can be a frightening and confusing emotion that can cloud what they are perceiving. Faith often can give you good tools to cope. Speaking to a spiritual advisor experienced with grief is like grabbing the end of a rope.

Don't forget to get your rest. Rest will keep you healthy and at your best. You need to get some sleep to help ease your mind. Sleep helps you from the stress to unwind. You have been through a lot so let your thoughts from you flee. Close your eyes and rest happily.

Staying healthy during the grieving process should be a priority. It will help you master your own life with authority. When you're coping with grief it's easy to stop caring about yourself. When your emotions are overwhelming it's easy to forget about your own wellbeing and put your health on the shelf. Eat nutritious meals, go out and take a walk or run. Get some vitamin D from the sun. Just be aware of your own health and your body's own health. Because in the long run, health is your greatest wealth.

Take care of your mind and your mental health. If you need help get it, no need to be stealth. Sometimes a counselor is what you need. Someone with experience to help you take the lead. Dealing with grief can sometimes be too much to bear. They can help with issues like depression, anxiousness, guilt and more if you dare. Looking after your mental health is probably one of the most important things you can do. Because your mind helps make you, you.

Finally, never ignore suicidal thoughts at all. Get the help you need there are hotlines to call. Check your local phone book for numbers to get professional help immediately. Suicide thoughts need to be handled expediently. ASAP because you and those you love are VIPS. No hesitation, no debating, no waiting.

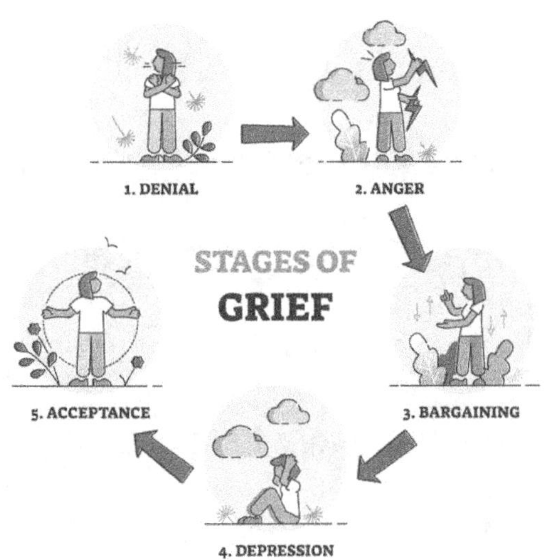

Mourning Affirmations

Death does not break the bond of love.

I recognize painful moments but know the will pass.

My life is a celebration of their life.

In my grief I have changed, but that is okay.

I can hold on to love and let go of grief.

Everything must come to an end.

The pain in my heart will heal.

I choose to feel at peace today.

I allow myself to feel my grief and let go.

I am taking my time to grieve.

I am not angry I am grieving.

I give myself time and space to feel all my feelings.

My heart feels lighter today.

Write Your Own Affirmations or Poems…

A FEW MORE POEMS

GRIEF

Grief is a heavy weight upon our hearts

It can make us feel so very low

But with time and understanding

We can heal and start to grow

We can't deny the pain and sadness

It's something we must face

But we can look ahead with optimism

And find a better place

We can learn to move forward

Though the hurtful memories remain

Letting go of the past

We can break the chains

We can look towards the future

And take what life can bring

With strength and courage

Our sorrow we can sing

For no matter how hard it may be

We can learn to heal our wounds

And with patience and compassion

Our joy can be soon resumed

WHEN GRIEF COMES KNOCKING

When grief comes knocking,

It can feel like a heavy weight,

Dragging us down into depths

We never thought we'd face.

But know that you are not alone,

In this dark and painful time.

There are others who have felt

The crushing weight of loss and sorrow,

And who have found a way to move forward,

One step at a time.

So take a deep breath and let it out,

Allow yourself to feel the pain,

But know that in time, it will subside,

And the memories of your loved one
Will bring a smile to your face once more.

Hold onto the love you shared,
And let it guide you through the days,
For though they may be gone,
Their love will always remain,
A shining light in your heart,
Forever shining bright.

So take comfort in the love you had,
And know that though they may be gone,
Their love will never fade,
It will always be a part of you,
A reminder of the happiness they brought,
And a source of strength to carry on.

GRIEF AND PAIN

In the midst of grief and pain,
It's hard to see the light again,
But know that your loved one lives on,

In the memories and love that now belong,

To you and all who knew them well,
In the stories and the tales they tell,
So hold on tight to all that's left,
And find the strength to keep on moving, step by
step.

For time may heal the deepest wounds,
And though the loss may still feel raw,
You'll find a way to carry on,
And your loved one will live on,

In all the things that you do,
In the love that you give and receive,
So hold on tight to what you knew,
And find the strength to keep on moving, through and
through.

THE LOSS OF A MOTHER

When a mother leaves this world,

It can feel like a piece of us is gone,
A part of our hearts forever torn.

But though she may no longer be with us,
Her love will always remain,
A guiding light in the darkest days,
A beacon of hope in the midst of pain.

So take comfort in the memories,
The moments that brought you joy,
For though she may be gone,
Her love will never die.

Hold onto the laughter and the tears,
The lessons she taught and the love she shared,
For these will always be a part of you,
A reminder of the gift she gave.

So hold your head up high,
And know that she is with you still,
Guiding you along life's path,

Forever in your heart and on your mind.

For though she may be gone,

Her love will never fade,

It will always be a part of you,

A source of strength and comfort,

As you navigate this world without her by your side.

THE STAGES OF GRIEF

In the first stage of grief, we feel stunned,

A punch to the gut, our breath is gone.

We can't believe that this has happened,

And we wish we could simply wake up from this bad

dream.

In the second stage, we feel pain,

A raw, aching wound that won't heal.

Tears flow freely, and we can't escape

The memories that bring us to our knees.

In the third stage, we feel anger,
A burning fire that consumes us whole.
We lash out at those around us,
Blaming them for what has happened.

In the fourth stage, we feel guilt,
A heavy weight that drags us down.
We blame ourselves for what has occurred,
Wishing we could change the past.

In the fifth stage, we feel bargaining,
A desperate attempt to regain control.
We make deals with the universe,
Pleading for another chance.

In the sixth stage, we feel depression,
A deep, dark hole that we can't escape.
We withdraw from the world around us,
Unable to find joy or meaning in anything.

In the final stage, we find acceptance,

A peace that comes from letting go.
We accept the reality of what has happened,
And we begin to move forward with our lives.

The stages of grief are not a straight line,
But a winding path that we must navigate.
But with time and support, we can heal,
And find a new sense of purpose and hope

THE LOSS OF A CHILD

In the darkness of the night,
A child has slipped away,
Leaving us with empty arms,
And a heart that's torn and frayed.

We hold onto memories,
Of the laughter and the love,
But it's hard to find the light,

In the midst of this despair.

We ask the question why,
Over and over again,
But no answer can bring comfort,
No words can ease the pain.

We'll never see them grow,
Or hear their voice again,
But in our hearts, they'll always be,
Our precious, cherished kin.

We'll carry them with us,
As we go on with our lives,
Holding tight to the love they gave,
And the joy they brought us inside.

Our child may be gone,
But their spirit lives on,
A reminder to cherish each day,
And to never be alone.

TO HEAL A BROKEN HEART

To heal a broken heart,

We must allow ourselves to grieve,

To cry and to feel the pain,

And to let our emotions run free.

It's not an easy journey,

And it may take some time,

But with the love and support of others,

We can begin to heal and to climb.

We must be kind to ourselves,

And give ourselves the space we need,

To process the loss and the pain,

And to plant the seeds of new growth and new

beginnings.

We must hold on to hope,

And believe that better days will come,

That the sun will shine again,

And that happiness will once more be ours to claim.

We are not alone in this journey,

For others have walked this path before,

And with their guidance and their love,

We can find the strength to heal and to soar.

THE ANGEL AND THE WIDOW

The angel came in the night,

As the widow lay in bed,

Her tears falling like rain,

As she grieved for her dead.

The angel whispered words of comfort,

As she stroked the widow's hair,

Reminding her of the love they shared,

And the memories they made together there.

The angel promised that her husband,
Was always by her side,
Watching over her and guiding her,
On her journey through this life.

The angel reminded the widow,
That she was not alone,
For the love they shared would never die,
And their bond would always be known.

With the angel's gentle touch,
And the warmth of her embrace,
The widow felt a sense of peace,
And the pain began to fade.

She knew that her husband,
Was always with her still,
And with the angel's guidance,
She would find the strength to heal.

HOPE IS THE LIGHT

Hope is the light that shines in the darkness,

A beacon of strength and courage,

A source of comfort and peace,

In times of great uncertainty and fear.

Hope is the spark that ignites our passion,

And drives us to pursue our dreams,

To overcome obstacles and challenges,

And to face each day with determination and grace.

Hope is the glue that holds us together,

When our world seems to be falling apart,

It gives us the strength to keep going,

And the courage to face whatever comes our way.

Hope is the fire that warms our hearts,

Even in the coldest and darkest of times,

It reminds us that there is always something to be

grateful for,

And that there is always a reason to keep fighting.

Hope is the foundation of our lives,

Without it, we would be lost,

So let us hold onto hope,

And let it guide us through this world,

As we chase our dreams, and live our lives to the

fullest.

ODE TO THE SANDMAN

The sandman comes in the night,

As we drift off to sleep,

He sprinkles magic dust,

To make our worries disappear.

He takes away the cares of the day,

And replaces them with sweet dreams,

He gives us the rest we need,

To wake up feeling refreshed and renewed.

He whispers soft lullabies,

As we drift off into a peaceful slumber,

He helps us to let go of our stress,

And to relax and unwind.

He is a friend and a guide,

In the world of dreams and imagination,

And with his help, we can escape,

From the struggles and the hardships of life.

So let us trust in the sandman,

And let him take away our fears,

For with his help, we can sleep soundly,

And wake up ready to take on the world.

A WORLD OF HAPPINESS AND LOVE

In this world of ours,

There is love and happiness,

It fills the air,

And surrounds us with warmth.

It's in the laughter of children,

And the smile on a friend's face,

It's in the embrace of loved ones,

And the feeling of home.

It's in the beauty of nature,

And the kindness of strangers,

It's in the moments of joy,

And the memories we treasure.

In this world of ours,

Love and happiness abound,

All we have to do,

Is open our hearts, and let it in.

For when we allow ourselves,

To be filled with love and happiness,

We can spread it to others,

And create a brighter, more beautiful world.

HOPE AND FAITH

Hope and faith,

Two shining lights,

Guiding us through the darkness,

And illuminating our path.

Hope is the spark,

That ignites our passion,

And drives us to chase our dreams,

And to pursue our goals.

Faith is the compass,

That points us in the right direction,

And helps us to trust,

In a greater power and purpose.

Together, hope and faith,

Are a powerful force,

They give us the strength,

To face whatever comes our way.

So let us hold onto hope,

And let faith guide us,

For with these two powerful allies,

We can achieve anything we set our minds to.

TURNING GRIEF INTO LOVE

Grief can be a heavy burden,

Weighing us down and dragging us under,

It can make us feel lost and alone,

And fill our hearts with pain and sorrow.

But there is a way,

To lighten the load,

To replace the grief in our hearts,

With love and hope and joy.

It starts with self-care,

Taking time to heal and to rest,

Surrounding ourselves with love and support,

And giving ourselves the space we need.

It continues with finding meaning,
In the things we do and the people we love,
Focusing on the good and the positive,
And letting go of the things that weigh us down.

And finally, it ends with acceptance,
Letting go of the past and the pain,
Embracing the present and the future,
And filling our hearts with love and light.

For when we replace the grief in our hearts,
With love and hope and joy,
We can find the strength to move forward,
And to live a happy and fulfilling life.

THE POWER OF ACCEPTANCE
The power of acceptance,
Is a force to be reckoned with,
It can free us from our chains,

And help us to find peace and contentment.

When we accept the things we cannot change,
We let go of the struggles and the fights,
We open ourselves up,
To the possibility of growth and change.

When we accept our flaws and our imperfections,
We learn to love ourselves,
We become kinder and gentler,
And we let go of the need to be perfect.

When we accept others,
For who they are and where they are in their journey,
We create space for connection and understanding,
And we build stronger, more loving relationships.

The power of acceptance,
Is a gift that we can give ourselves,
And when we embrace it,
We open the door to a happier and more fulfilling life.

THE POWER OF FORGIVENESS

The power of forgiveness,

Is a gift that we can give,

To ourselves and to others,

It's a way to let go of anger and pain.

Forgiveness isn't about condoning,

The actions of those who have hurt us,

It's about letting go of the grudge,

And finding peace and healing within.

When we forgive,

We release ourselves from the shackles,

Of bitterness and resentment,

And we open ourselves up to love and joy.

Forgiveness isn't always easy,

It can be a difficult and painful process,

But in the end, it's worth it,

For the freedom and the healing it brings.

So let us practice forgiveness,
In our own lives and in the world,
For when we do,
We create a brighter, more loving future.

DO NOT WEEP BESIDE MY GRAVE

Do not stand at my grave and weep,
For I am not there, I do not sleep.
I am the gentle breeze that blows through the trees,
I am the bright stars that twinkle in the night sky.

I am the memories you hold dear in your heart,
The love that we shared, that will never part.
I am the laughter and the joy we shared,

I am the peace that fills your soul, when you are
scared.

So do not stand at my grave and weep,
For I am not really gone, I am just asleep.
I am the love that surrounds you, always near,
I am the hope that comforts you, wiping away your
tears.

I am the light that guides you through the darkness,
I am the strength that helps you carry on.
So do not stand at my grave and weep,
For I am not really gone, I am just gone before.
I am the love that lives on, forevermore.

Do not stand at my grave and weep,
For I am not there, I do not sleep.
I am a thousand winds that blow,
I am the diamond glints on snow.

I am the sunlight on ripened grain,

I am the gentle autumn rain.
When you awaken in the morning's hush,
I am the swift uplifting rush

Of quiet birds in circled flight.
I am the soft stars that shine at night.
Do not stand at my grave and cry,
I am not there, I did not die.

Though I may be gone, my love will remain,
A constant force that will ease your pain.
So do not stand at my grave and weep,
But find solace in the memories we keep.

DO NOT BE SAD WHEN I DIE

Do not be sad when I die, my love,
For death is just a part of life.
It's a journey we all must take,
A path that leads to endless light.

Though I may no longer be by your side,

My spirit will always be near.

I'll be the gentle breeze on your skin,

The soothing sound in your ear.

Do not be sad when I die, my dear,

For I will always be with you.

In the memories we've made together,

In the love that we've shared and knew.

So hold on to the happy times,

And the love that we shared so true.

And know that I'll always be with you,

Even when this life is through.

For I will live on through the memories we share.

In the love we've shared and the laughter we've

shared,

I'll always be with you, even if I'm not there.

Though my body may be gone, my spirit will remain,

A constant presence in the joy and love we've made.

So do not be sad when I die,

But find comfort in the love we shared and never fade.

I'll be watching over you from above,

Guiding and protecting you with all my love.

So do not be sad when I die,

But hold on to the love we shared and never say goodbye.

REMEMBERING THE WONDERFUL MEMORIES

Today we remember your life and celebrate all the wonderful memories we have,

The laughter we shared, the love we gave.

We think back on all the moments that meant so much,

The holidays, the birthdays, the times we were out of touch.

We remember the stories you told, the lessons you
taught,
The way you always knew just what we needed, no
matter what.
You were more than just a loved one, you were a
friend,
And the love you shared will never have to end.

So today we remember your life and all the joy it
brought,
And celebrate the memories that will always be
sought.
We hold you close in our hearts, though you're not
here,
And the love you left behind will always be near.

We may be grieving, but we are also thankful,
For the time we had with you, so precious and grand.
So today we remember your life and all that it meant,
And celebrate the memories that we'll always resent.

Today we remember your life,

And celebrate all the wonderful memories we have.

The moments we shared, the love we made,

All the joy and laughter that we had.

We recall the kindness and warmth you brought,

The way you touched the lives of those around.

Your light shone bright, it never dimmed,

And in our hearts, it will always be found.

So let us raise a glass and offer a toast,

To a life well lived, a love that never fades.

Today we remember your life and celebrate,

All the wonderful memories we have made.

Though you may be gone, your spirit remains,

A constant presence that eases our pain.

So let us hold on to the love you left behind,

And know that you are always with us, in our hearts

intertwined.

WE WILL CHERISH OUR MEMORIES OF YOU

We will cherish the memories we have of you,

And remember your amazing life.

The way you lived, the love you gave,

All the joy and laughter that filled our days.

You touched the lives of those you met,

With kindness, warmth, and a generous heart.

Your light shone bright, it never dimmed,

And in our hearts, it will always be a part.

So today we honor your memory,

And all the wonderful moments we shared.

We will cherish the memories we have of you,

And remember the love that never fades.

We will cherish the memories we have of you,

And remember your amazing life.

The way you loved, the way you cared,

Your spirit bright, your spirit fair.

You touched so many lives in your time,
Leaving behind a love that will always shine.
Your light will never fade, it will always glow,
A beacon of hope that we can always know.

So let us hold on to the memories we have,
And find comfort in the love you gave.
We will cherish the memories we have of you,
And remember your amazing life, forever true.

DON'T CRY BECAUSE ITS OVER

Don't cry because it's over,
Smile because it happened.
Remember the joy and love we shared,
The memories we made, never to be compared.

Life is a journey, full of ups and downs,

But through it all, love surrounds.

Hold on to the memories, let them fill your heart,

For they are the gifts that will never part.

So don't cry because it's over,

Smile because it happened.

Life is a precious gift, one to be cherished,

So hold on to the love and memories, never to be

perished.

Though we may say goodbye, the love remains,

A constant presence that eases the pains.

So don't cry because it's over,

Smile because it happened,

and the love we shared will always be a part of you.

Don't cry because it's over,

Smile because it happened.

For the memories we made, the love we shared,

Are things that can never be taken.

Though you may be gone, your spirit remains,

A constant presence that eases the pain.

So don't cry because it's over,

But find joy in the memories we've made together.

Remember the laughter, the joy, the fun,

The love that we shared, it will always be won.

Don't cry because it's over,

But smile because it happened, forever in our hearts.

Though we may be apart in body, we'll always be

one,

Bound together by the love we have won.

So don't cry because it's over,

But smile because it happened, and remember the

love we shared.

A TRAIL OF BEAUTIFUL MEMORIES

Wherever a beautiful soul has been,

There is a trail of beautiful memories.

The moments we shared, the love we made,

All the joy and laughter, they will never fade.

For a beautiful soul leaves behind a light,

That shines on in the hearts of those in its sight.

A constant presence that eases the pain,

A love that forever remains.

So let us hold on to the memories we have,

And find comfort in the love that was shared.

Wherever a beautiful soul has been,

There is a trail of beautiful memories, forever in our

hearts.

Wherever a beautiful soul has been,

There is a trail of beautiful memories.

A tapestry of love and laughter,

A path of joy and love that will always be.

Though you may be gone, your spirit remains,

A constant presence that eases the pain.

Your beautiful soul has left a trail of love,

A path of memories that we are grateful of.

So let us hold on to the memories we have,

And find comfort in the love you gave.

Wherever a beautiful soul has been,

There is a trail of beautiful memories, forever true.

ALWAYS ON MY MIND, FOREVER IN MY HEART

Always on my mind, forever in my heart,

You are a love that will never part.

A constant presence that fills my soul,

A love that makes me whole.

Though you may be gone, your spirit remains,

A guiding light that eases the pain.

You are always on my mind, forever in my heart,

A love that will never depart.

I hold on to the memories we made,

The laughter, the joy, the love that never fades.
You are always on my mind, forever in my heart,
A love that keeps us never apart.

Always on my mind, forever in my heart,
You are a love that will never depart.
A constant presence that fills my days,
A guiding light that never fades.

Though you may be gone, your spirit remains,
A constant force that eases the pains.
Your love is a gift that I will always keep,
A treasure that I will always hold dear.

So let me hold on to the memories we have made,
And find comfort in the love we shared.
Always on my mind, forever in my heart,
You are a love that I will always hold close, forever in
my soul.

JOURNEY THROUGH THE SEVEN STAGES OF GRIEF

The seven stages of grief, a journey we must take

When someone we love has passed away

Each stage a step on the road to healing

A path that is winding and often revealing

First comes the shock, a numbness inside

A disbelief that our loved one has died

We try to deny it, to push it away

But the truth remains, no matter what we say

Next comes the pain, a deep and overwhelming ache

As we come to terms with our loved one's fate

We may feel anger, at the world or at them

For leaving us behind, alone to fend

Bargaining is the third stage, a desperate plea

To turn back time, to make things as they used to be

We may try to make deals with a higher power

But ultimately, we must accept the hour

Depression follows, a heavy weight on our hearts
As we struggle to find joy in life's simple arts
We may feel isolated and alone
But it's important to reach out, to find a new tone

The sixth stage brings a glimmer of hope
As we begin to find ways to cope
We may start to find meaning in our loss
We may even find new ways to toss

The final stage is acceptance, a peace within
We've come to understand, we must begin
To live our lives without our loved one there
But their memory will always be with us, we'll always
care

The seven stages of grief, a journey we must take
But with time and support, we'll eventually wake
To a new reality, a new way of life

One filled with love and hope and light.

SAYING GOODBYE

Saying goodbye is never easy
It's a pain that cuts so deep
It feels like a piece of you is missing
As if your heart has been ripped from your chest

But know that you are not alone
In your grief and your sorrow
There are others who have walked this road
And found a way to face tomorrow

It may feel like the darkness will never lift
Like the pain will never subside
But there is hope on the horizon
A glimmer of light to guide

Take things one day at a time

And don't be afraid to reach out
To friends and family for support
They'll be there for you, no doubt

It's okay to cry, to feel the weight
Of the loss you carry inside
But know that your loved one is at peace
And they'll always be by your side

Hold onto the memories you shared
The love that will never fade
And know that your loved one is watching
From a place where they will always be safe

Saying goodbye is never easy
But it's a part of life we all must do
And though it may seem like the end
It's really a new beginning for you.

Saying goodbye is never easy
It's a heartache that cuts deep

But the love we shared will never die
It will always be ours to keep

Though the pain may feel unbearable
And the road ahead seems long
Remember that you are not alone
And you are loved and belong

Take comfort in the memories
Of all the love and joy you shared
Hold onto them tight and close
For they will always be with you, always cared

And know that your loved one is at peace
Their suffering now at an end
They will always be with you in spirit
Watching over you, loving you, and then

So grieve and mourn and cry
But also find solace in the thought
That your loved one is now at rest

And the love you have will never be forgot

FINDING STRENGTH IN THE DARK

When the darkness surrounds you
And the pain feels too much to bear
Remember that you are strong
And you have the courage to care

You may feel lost and alone
But you are not, not by a long shot
There are those who love and support you
And will never leave you to rot

Take comfort in their presence
In their love and their light
They will help guide you through
This darkest of nights

And know that your loved one
Is always with you, in spirit and in heart

Their love will give you strength
And help you through this difficult part

So hold onto hope and faith
In the goodness and the love that still exists
And take the time you need to heal
For you are worthy and you will not be dismissed

Finding strength in the dark, when all seems lost
Can seem like an impossible task
But know that within you is a light
That will guide you through the night

In the depths of your grief and pain
It can be hard to find your way
But take comfort in the fact
That you are strong, and you can act

To honor your loved one and find peace
To keep their memory alive, to never cease
To love and be loved, to find joy once more

To open your heart, to love and to explore

So take one step at a time, be kind to yourself
And know that it's okay to not be okay
Reach out for support, for a comforting hand
And know that you are loved, understand

That you are not alone in this journey of grief
That others have walked this path, found relief
And though the road ahead may be long
You will find strength, you will be strong.

GRIEFS UNEXPECTED GIFTS

Grief's unexpected gifts, it may seem strange
To think of them as such, in this time of pain
But in the midst of our sorrow and despair
There are moments of grace, of love, of care

We may discover new strengths within ourselves
That we never knew existed before

We may find a renewed sense of purpose
In the love and memories we still keep and adore

We may also find a deeper appreciation
For the time we have, for the present moment
And a newfound gratitude for the people
Who love and support us, who are a true testament

To the power of love, to the resilience of the human
heart
So don't be afraid to grieve and to feel
All the emotions that come, that are real

For in time, you will find a way to heal
To find joy once more, to love and to feel
The unexpected gifts that grief can bring
A new perspective, a new everything.

Grief's unexpected gifts, a concept hard to grasp
But know that amidst the pain and the tears
There are things to be gained, things to be learned

That can bring new growth, that can be earned

Like the gift of perspective, of what truly matters
Of the preciousness of life, and the love that flatters
Like the gift of compassion, of empathy and care
For others who are hurting, who are in despair

Like the gift of resilience, of strength and endurance
Of the ability to adapt and to mature
Like the gift of appreciation, of gratitude and grace
For the moments we shared, for the time and the
place

So though it may be hard to see
Grief's unexpected gifts, they can be
A source of comfort and hope and love
In the darkest of times, from up above

THE JOURNEY OF GRIEF

The journey of healing, a road we all must take

When a loved one has left us, for heaven's gates
It's a journey filled with ups and downs
And sometimes, a feeling of being lost and found

But know that you are not alone
On this journey, this path of your own
There are others who have walked this way
And found a way to heal, to make it through each day

It's a journey that takes time and patience
And sometimes, a lot of tears and frustration
But know that you are strong, and you have the
power
To heal and to love, in this new hour

So take it one day at a time, and be kind to yourself
And know that it's okay to not be okay
Reach out for support, for a comforting hand
And know that you are loved, understand

That you are on a journey, a journey of healing

And though it may be hard, and sometimes revealing
You will find your way, you will find your peace
And your loved one's love will always be with you,
never cease

So hold onto hope, and keep moving forward
The journey of healing, it can be a challenge, a
reward
But know that you are loved, and you are not alone
On this journey of grief, on this journey of home.

FINDING PEACE IN THE PAIN

Finding peace in the pain, a challenge we all face
When a loved one is gone, and we're left in their
place
It's a journey that takes time and patience
And sometimes, a lot of tears and frustration

But know that peace can be found
In the memories, in the love that surrounds

In the moments we shared, in the love that remains
In the knowledge that our loved one is at peace, and
not in pain

So take comfort in the thought
That they are at rest, and their love is still sought
By those who knew them and loved them so
And will always carry their memory, wherever they go

And know that it's okay to grieve and to mourn
To feel the pain, to feel forlorn
But also know that it's important to find
A way to heal, a way to be kind

To yourself and to others, to love and to give
To find joy in the present, and a way to live
Without your loved one by your side
But with their memory always in your heart and mind

So hold onto hope, and keep moving forward

Finding peace in the pain, it can be a challenge, a
reward
But know that you are loved, and you are not alone
In this journey of grief, in this journey of home.

It may take time, and it may be hard
But know that you are strong, and you have the heart
To overcome this grief, this loss and this pain
To find a way to love, to find a way to gain

A new perspective, a new way of living
A way to find meaning, a way of giving
Back to the world, back to the ones you love
A way to keep your loved one's memory alive, above

So don't give up, and don't lose hope
There is peace to be found, there is a way to cope
With the pain and the grief, and the loneliness too
Just take it one day at a time, and know that you are
not alone
In your journey of healing, in your journey of love.

MORE EXTRA CONTENT

Because the pandemic has affected all our lives, and many people are still grieving, I've included a few poems in this edition of the book.

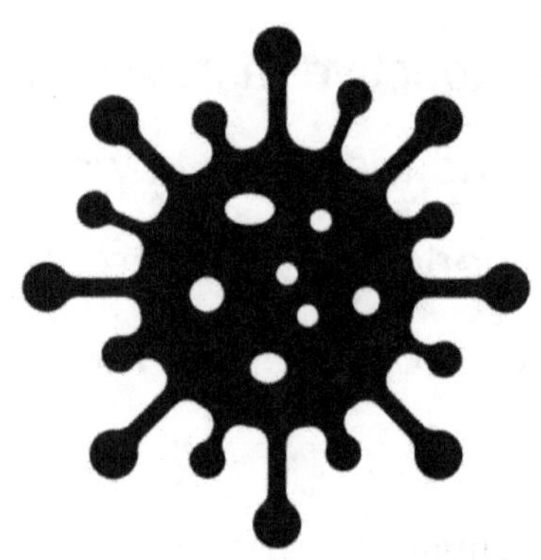

The Sun is Shining

The sun is shining, it's a beautiful day,

but many on this planet remain locked away.

Not through any fault of their own,

They are told to remain alone.

The elderly hiding from a virus unseen,

Those with health problems dodging a virus so mean.

A virulent strain that preys upon the weak.

Tick, tock, tick, tock, there goes another week.

The clock ticks slowly as they wait,

Nowhere to go, no important date.

Tick, tock, tick, tock,

Perhaps they'll mend a sock.

Tick, tock, tick, tock,

In their rocker they rock.

A knock on the door, a package left with love.

Brings peace to the heart of a caged dove.

The goodness you share with those alone,

Can be as simple as picking up a phone.

It only takes a small act to do a great deed.

So, make some plans to help someone in need.

The Earth Somberly Said

The wild animal mournfully said,

It's because of mankind, I'm almost dead.

It's getting harder for me to breathe this way,

Stacked with others in an Asian meat market we lay.

The virus worried he was about to lose his host,

Developed an ingenious plan to infect the most.

A clever mutation soon was unfurled,

Wreaking havoc on an unsuspecting world.

The politicians confidently said,

It's because of this virus so many are dead.

It'll take trillions of dollars to heal this plague,

The rest of their plans were quite vague.

Many panicked people on a shopping spree,

Worrying about loved ones, but a few were in glee.

Some simply called it a thinning of the heard.

While the majority said that's just absurd.

We can beat this virus became the cry of the nations,

Just lock yourselves in and steer clear of social
relations.

Still those that thought only of themselves didn't care less,

Partied and mocked ordinances and continued the mess.

And, slowly one, by one they caught the virus.

The hospital resources they took up left a great stain.

Because of their selfishness many more died in vain.

Humanity at Test

Your humanity and concern

for others is at test.

Prepare for the worst,

but expect the best.

No need to hoard

and leave others without.

If you're not going to use it,

from your shopping cart leave it out.

Prepare but purchase

only what you'll need,

don't let your heart be filled with greed.

Remember the less fortunate,

whom shop week by week.

Exposing themselves to this virus in exchange for
simple necessities they seek.

If we all work together and do what we can

for those in our community.

We will fortify each other

and from any crisis develop immunity.

The Wake-Up Call

The politicians continued to argue back and forth,

Meanwhile the virus spread east, west, south and
north.

Stimulate the economy, prevent economic collapse,

We are in uncharted territory and need to fill in the
gaps.

Small businesses are suffering, the stores are getting
bare,

As for the sick and elderly, how much would it cost
us to care?

Shall we care about people or power,

This seemed to be the question of the hour.

If the youth don't get the virus,

Should we be making such a fuss?

If they don't work our country declines,

Perhaps we should rewrite the health guidelines?

Bills needed to be passed urgently, could both sides be a team?

Not exactly they proved, non-partisan politics is just a dream.

They continued to argue putting their own needs first,

Then weeded through every idea, pulling out the worst.

With the decisions they make, many lives they could save.

And the wrong ones could send many lives to the grave.

Eventually though both sides got what they wanted.

But did they do enough or will their conscious constantly be haunted?

No Immunity

I could care less if I caught it and spread it to the old, said the rebellious teen.

There are too many old folks in the world, and they are behind the times and mean.

Their negativity and dogmatic views from the earth we need to purge.

The others chimed in compassionate socialism must be the new surge.

The old man hearing things like this day in and day out,

Was more determined than ever to save the world from the devout.

He rattled out his battle cry in front of his computer once more,

Effortlessly, as if he had said it thousands of times before.

He opened with his usual speech explaining what the virus was,

and continued telling others just what the virus does.

He stated, most of us have immunity to the common flu,

however, Covid19 is novel which means its new.

Its RNA sequencing is for animals not us,

This is why everyone is making such a fuss.

Human bodies do not recognize it, so all will get sick,

Passing it on to each other extremely quick.

For some it will be symptomless or like a mild cold,

But it's extremely dangerous if your unhealthy or old.

Not only can it infect people at an alarming rate,

It can sometimes mutate rapidly into another state.

Now there are two versions, the S and L strain,

Both attack the lungs and breathing with disdain.

This is what makes it difficult to produce a vaccine,

Because today it could be one thing, tomorrow something unseen.

These things have caused this systemic epidemic to become pandemic.

Pandering and meandering throughout the world stated the ancient academic.

At the end of his live video on his YouTube feed.

He added in his disclaimer for his viewers to heed.

I do not wish to alarm you, you just need to prepare,

There are many ways you can help stop this, if you dare.

Wash your hands, self-isolate, take your vitamins and exercise more,

He then said goodbye to his followers and walked out his office door.

He looked out the window, which was the portal for his cell,

And sadly, watched the Spring Break crowd on the beach raising hell.

Almost Going Outside

He sat on the couch and at night he went to bed,

Grocery delivery services were what kept him fed.

Minutes turned to hours, hours turned to days,

Days turned to weeks, while home he stays.

I can't take it anymore, I'm going insane.

I'm wasting my life away he said with disdain.

If each day is the first day of the rest of my life,

From the looks of things my future is already filled with strife.

How can I follow my dreams as they say?

Or live life to the fullest as I hideaway?

Enough of this he stated with a lion's roar,

I'm just going to be brave and go out the door.

That's right I'm going to do it, step, by step,

He gave himself an inspirational talk with pep.

But first I need to prepare as a responsible person would,

I need rubber gloves, a mask, Purell and a plastic coat with a hood.

Lysol, germicidal towelettes and some chemistry goggles.

But wait there's more, what am I missing? His mind boggles.

Oh yeah, first take all my vitamins and extra doses of C, D and Zinc,

Come on brain, what else is there, I need to think!

Was it 6 feet away from people or 10 feet to avoid an aerosol spray?

And if 10 people are in a group, the eleventh needs to walk away?

Do I need a plastic bag for the handle on the gasoline pump?

Because if I use my glove only, I'd have to toss it in the dump.

What if I touch my face with my contaminated glove?

What if my mask slips down from my nose, it's perched above?

What if I go outside and catch it and others catch it from me?

Is it worth the chance simply to be free?

Just then came the familiar knock on the door he knew at once,

The grocery delivery service was here with his lunch.

Grocery delivery services were what kept him fed.

He sat on the couch and at night he went to bed.

Helping Them Breathe

Under the covers, protected from harm.

Secretly wishing she could avoid the alarm.

Safe in her bed, eyes still stained with tears.

Safe in her home, miles from her fears.

The alarm now buzzes relentlessly loud,

Wake up, wake up, time to put on your shroud.

There are lives that are depending on you,

It's almost time to do what you must do.

No time for hesitating, no time for debating,

From beginning to end, do the rounds again,

It's your turn to care for them all,

It's time to heed societies call.

Moms, dads, sons, daughters waiting to be seen.

The hours are getting shorter, less time for sleep between.

So many people waiting in rooms side by side,

Waiting for her the alarm cried.

She rolls over and gets out of bed.

Gaining inner strength to forge ahead.

The Medias Constant Barrage

The medias constant barrage hit the man like a brick,

It soon felt to him like the whole world was sick,

The news kept warning him to stay inside,

But to him, he thought it foolish, real men don't hide.

Haachoo…

Huh? Did the bank teller over there just sneeze?

Perhaps he has the Corona disease?

Ahem-hem…

Why did the mailman just clear his throat?

Perhaps he caught the disease carrying letters from remote.

Couggghhh, couggghhh…

Oh my God he said aloud when he heard the grocery bagger cough.

"Cover your mouth" he yelled, with an angry scoff.

His constant pandemic paranoia perplexed everyone,

He just kept getting angrier in his world of one.

He hit the breaking point one day and said enough,

He set out to learn everything about this virus so tough.

He went to all the recommended websites that he should,

He read up on the virus until he understood.

He learned the symptoms and precautions to take,

And, with it came a sense of peace as he was fully awake.

Feeling like an expert he told his friends about the disease,

Bringing calmness and understanding to help them feel at ease.

His friends told others, passing along good information instead of fears,

A simple message that spread around and helped saved lives and tears

Out of the Darkness

Out of the darkness and still of the night.

Into the day yet out of sight.

A virus crept into our lives like a thief.

Many prepared some stood paralyzed in disbelief.

A world turned upside down,

exposing our fears and insecurities.

Some whom appeared strong became weak.

Some whom appeared weak became strong.

Faced with a decision to worry about ourselves,

or open our hearts to care.

To elevate the panic

or face our fears head on if we dare.

and, to the countless people who heeded this call.

To the valiant persons who gave it their all.

We salute your sacrifice to keep us from harm.

Whether caring for the sick or delivering food from the farm.

To all the essential workers, and volunteers too.

You've become the light to help see us through.

Bringing humanity from the insanity,

Calmness from the calamity, you are all heroes.